STRENGTH TO LOVE

GREG AMUNDSON

STRENGTH TO LOVE

Copyright © 2020 Greg Amundson

ISBN 978-0-578-79032-9

By Greg Amundson

3703 Portola Drive, Santa Cruz, CA 95060

www.GregoryAmundson.com

Edited by Cindy Bond

Layout and Design by Katie Sanchez

Artwork by Karl Eagleman

The author has done his best to articulate and illustrate God's Word by means of prayer, meditation and contemplation. Italics or brackets within a Scripture are the author's own emphasis.

Published by:
Eagle Rise Publishing, Virginia Beach, VA.
EagleRisePublishing.com
Printed and bound in the USA and UK on acid-free paper.
Additional books can be purchased through Amazon.

PRAISE FOR THE WORK OF GREG AMUNDSON

"Greg Amundson is a true warrior leader and monk. His deep commitment to his faith, and ability to communicate that faith through his passion for the warrior mindset, is unparalleled. *The Good Soldier* is another lighted path that Greg has provided for those searching for Truth."
— ***Mark Divine***, U.S. Navy SEAL (Retired) *New York Times* bestselling author of
The Way of the SEAL, Unbeatable Mind and *Staring Down the Wolf*

"Greg's ability to transcend boundaries and speak to the essence of spirituality is profound and encouraging."
— ***Scott McEwen***, #1 *New York Times* bestselling co-author of *American Sniper*;
national bestselling *Sniper Elite* series, and the new *Camp Valor* series of novels

"I often tell people at my seminars, 'We don't need more Buddhists in the world, we need more Buddhas. We don't need more Christians, we need more Christ-like beings.' And such is the case with my amazing, breathing brother Greg Amundson. He's not one of those wishy-washy, praise the Lord, in-your-face, superficial Christians: He is a former SWAT Operator, DEA Special Agent, U.S. Army Captain, and CrossFit athlete and coach. He is a spiritual warrior, and he carries God in his heart. Greg's sermons, lectures and books teach the principles of spiritual development that can change your life."
— ***Dan Brulé***, world renowned lecturer and international
bestselling author of *Just Breathe*

"Greg Amundson is the epitome of a modern day warrior. He leads in all aspects of his life: as a warrior, as a Christian, and as a fitness expert. He writes with magical simplicity, yet is rigorous in his research and reasoning. As a leadership and motivation coach, when I need my own motivation I look to Greg Amundson. His track record of proving the validity of his message in his own life, and the lives that his message touches, is astounding."
— ***Jason Redman***, Navy SEAL (Retired) and *New York Times* bestselling author
of *The Trident: the Forging and Reforging of a Navy SEAL Leader*

"Greg Amundson is one of the most prolific author's and speakers of our time, and his work will profoundly bless your life."

— **Dr. Gabrielle Lyon**, DO, Special Operations, Task Force Dagger

"Greg Amundson's new book *The Good Soldier* contains a visionary message on leadership, self-mastery, and walking the path of a modern day warrior. This is a profound and encouraging read that has reinvigorated my desire to be of service to others. Hooyah!"

— **Joe De Sena**, Spartan Founder & CEO and #1 *New York Times* bestselling author of *Spartan Up!*

"Greg Amundson has the ability to weave the warrior mindset and biblical message in a way that cuts to my heart. His sermons and books encourage me to put God first, strive for self-mastery, and be of greater service to others."

— **Jay Dobyns**, ATF Special Agent (Retired) *New York Times* bestselling author of *No Angel* and *Catching Hell*

ALSO BY GREG AMUNDSON

Published Books

Your Wife is NOT Your Sister
Robertson Publishing – 2012

Firebreather Fitness
(with TJ Murphy) Velo Press – 2016

The Warrior and The Monk
Robertson Publishing – 2018

Above All Else – A Year of Increasing Wisdom, Stature, and Favor
Eagle Rise Publishing – 2018

Victory! – A Practical Guide to Forging Eternal Fitness
Eagle Rise Publishing – 2019

The Good Soldier
Eagle Rise Publishing – 2019

Knowledge of the Most High
Eagle Rise Publishing – 2020

CrossFit® Journal Articles

A Chink in My Armor
Coaching the Mental Side of CrossFit
CrossFit HQ – 2851 Research Park Drive, Santa Cruz, CA.
Diet Secrets of the Tupperware Man Vol. I
Diet Secrets of the Tupperware Man Vol. II
Forging Elite Leadership
Good Housekeeping Matters
How to Grow a Successful Garage Gym
Training Two Miles to Run 100

ACKNOWLEDGMENTS

First and foremost, I am exceedingly grateful for the everlasting love and embrace of God and His Son, Jesus Christ. For my beloved parents, Raymond and Julianne Amundson, who encouraged me from a young age to develop my mind, body, and spirit in such a manner that I could be of greater service to others. A great deal of appreciation is extended to Brooklyn Taylor for her brilliant layout and design contributions to this book. I am indebted to the great pastoral mentors and educators whose leadership has deeply influenced my understanding of doctrine and theology: Mark Divine, Dan Brulé, Ken Gray (in memoriam), Chaplain Richard Johnson, Pastor Dave Hicks, Dr. Deepak Chopra, Raja John Bright, Dr. Gary Tuck, Dr. Steve Korch, Dr. Adam Nigh, Pastor René Schlaepfer, Pastor Max Lucado, Bishop Robert Barron, and Dr. Charles Stanley. Finally, to the students and exemplary teaching staff at Western Seminary, may you continue to experience "Gospel Centered Transformation" in every area of your life.

DEDICATION

"Children, obey your parents in everything,
for this pleases the Lord."

— Colossians 3:20

This book is dedicated in loving memory
to my mom and dad, who provided me with the greatest
example of a "Heart like Christ" I have ever known.

"God is more worthy of your pursuit, attention, and love than
all the other passions of the world combined."

— Dr. Raymond Amundson

"God is entirely devoted to your personal advancement."

— Julianne Amundson

TABLE OF CONTENTS

FOREWORD

FOREWORD

WHEN I WAS FIRST INTRODUCED to CrossFit® in the early 2000's, like many others, I began to dig deep into the impressive workout videos on the website. As a collegiate strength and conditioning coach I was well versed in the Olympic lifts, interval training, and various strength exercises. However, I had never witnessed what I was seeing in these videos. These "regular people" were mixing all of the above in an effort to develop high-level functional fitness. They were training at an unimaginable pace while also executing great technique. How was this possible? Was this safe? Who were these people? These were questions I asked myself as I continued to explore this new way of training.

One of the most impressive people in these videos was Greg Amundson. I remember wondering how this guy became so fit. He displayed amazing commitment to his physical training along with his impressive discipline in nutrition. He was the "Tupperware Man." This was so motivational to me and it encouraged me to push harder in my own areas of discipline.

It was no surprise to learn later that Greg is a fellow believer in Jesus Christ. Many people assume Christians are soft, weak people. This assumption is unfortunate. One reason I believe the assumption is made is due to our discussion of grace, love, and mercy. These concepts sound soft on the surface. A person who is committed to grace, love, and mercy sounds like he is probably a pushover. It certainly does not sound like someone who would train to the point of failure, laying on the ground after a workout, gasping for breath. The person who trains with that kind of intensity sounds more like a person who would say "no mercy."

Without a true knowledge of the Christian faith, I understand the assumption of a Christian being soft, or weak. However, when someone truly commits to following Jesus Christ, this perspective changes quickly. A true believer of Jesus Christ is attempting to follow the most disciplined person to ever walk the planet. This leads to a life marked by standards of excellence. It is a life defined by strength. But where does this strength come from?

The good news of Jesus Christ teaches us to live by the high standard of sacrificial love. His gift of salvation motivates us to love others by this same high standard. Instead of a weak, soft life, God calls us to a strong, joy-filled life that elevates others above ourselves. This takes enormous strength, so it can only come from a source greater than ourselves.

Greg's new book *Strength To Love* will point you to your true source of strength. Open up God's Word, and share what you learn with others. To this effect, I pray that you find the 12 lessons in Greg's book helpful in understanding God's Word as you seek His strength to love those around you.

CHIP PUGH
Discipleship Minister & Leadership Coach
Collegeside Church of Christ
Co-Founder of Faith RXD

INTRODUCTION

INTRODUCTION

IN DECEMBER 2001, I WALKED a small CrossFit® Box, experienced the thrill of my first workout, crumbled into a heap on the floor, and thought that I was going to die. Although physically crushed, my spirit was elated—by the grace of God, I had uncovered the Holy Grail of fitness, and my life would never be the same.

After 20 years of service within the CrossFit community, I think I am finally starting to understand the greater implications of what makes the program so compelling. In the *physical realm*, rather than a speculative approach to defining CrossFit, the methodology can be understood in a practical, observable, and objective manner. By looking closely at the governing principles of CrossFit— its inherent focus on constantly varied functional movement performed at high intensity—we can develop a sound grasp for the magnificence of the program.

Although the physical rewards of CrossFit are extremely gratifying, I often wonder if there yet remains an untapped reservoir of potential that transcends the temporal "score on a whiteboard" or rank on a leaderboard. In other words, I propose that the CrossFit community is primed to forge more than just physical adaptation, and that we must challenge any preconceived notion that CrossFit is limited to the objective realm of our senses. It is high time that our community started to focus on the *spiritual realm*.

You see my friends, if we restrict our definition of CrossFit to the physical expression of the program, we become subject to the longstanding admonishment that "people look at the outward appearance, but God looks at the heart" (1 Samuel 16:7). Nearly a lifetime of athletic training has led me to understand that what happens within our minds and hearts is truly the greatest expression of our ability to satisfy the purpose of CrossFit: *to increase in work capacity across broad time and modal domains*. However, unlike the physical skills we learn and practice within the Box, the Bible teaches that there are some things we cannot do on our own. In the gym, we need a spotter—in life, we need a Savior.

By way of illustration, consider the attendees at the CrossFit Level I Course: they are taught that the key to increasing in work capacity (i.e., going faster in

"Fran") is adhering to the formula of moving large loads for long distances, very quickly! And how is this achieved? The disciplined athlete learns they must follow one of the universal principles of functional movement: the athlete is instructed to accelerate the object through a relay of contractions from *core to extremity*. This powerful and controlled series of contractions allows the athlete to produce power: power is defined as intensity, and intensity is the *independent variable most commonly associated with maximizing the rate of return on favorable adaptation.*

And herein we arrive at the cornerstone of the biblical solution to every problem that we will ever face. We must focus on the *spiritual equivalent* of the *physical independent variable*, which is our *True Core*—reconciliation with God through a saving relationship with Jesus Christ. When we "seek first the Kingdom of God," we allow for God's grace to positively and constructively influence all the extremities of our life (Matthew 6:33). In other words, when God is in first place (*our Core*), then all the other pieces of our life fit perfectly into place (*the extremity*). In the words of C. S. Lewis, "When we look for Christ we will find Him, and with Him everything else thrown in."[1]

Here is the main point I want to make: God is the independent variable of our life. By grace through faith in Christ, the believer is reconciled with God, indwelt by the Holy Spirit, and equipped to maximize our life in a supernatural way (Ephesians 2:8–9; Acts 1:8, 2:4–39).

In the event it is not already painfully obvious, I love the methodology of CrossFit and everything that the community stands for. However, I also fear that for many people—myself included—CrossFit can become a form of idolatry. Biblically speaking, "idol worship" means to put something other than God into the rightful place reserved for God alone. If God is that to which we give all our time, energy, thought, and attention, then many of us are clearly engaged in worshipping things that are the idol of our own creation. When idolatry happens in any degree, our entire world begins to revolve around what we worship; speaking from experience, this inherently sinful act of disobedience to God can creep into our life in unexpected and ensnaring ways.

---

[1] C. S. Lewis, *Mere Christianity* (New York, NY: Collier Books, 1963), p. 175.

That being said, God has an amazing way of putting Christian leaders in the right place, at the right time, to help change the course of history. I believe that CrossFit athletes can be a catalyst for the Gospel message right between the four walls of their CrossFit Box—and it's my prayer that this book can help you accomplish that awesome mission. In other words, you can preach the Gospel to the micro-nation of the CrossFit community right in your own backyard.

When preaching to the micro-nation inside the Box, it is imperative that Christian leaders are able to relate the Gospel within the context and framework of the CrossFit culture. As a first step, we need to ground ourselves in a solid understanding of the Bible and systematic theology. Biblical revelation treats God's attributes and qualities not in a speculative way, but rather in an objective and practical manner[2]. There is a vital connection between the God of the Holy Bible and the way we are called to relate to Him. Furthermore, there is a direct relationship between who God is, what God does as revealed within His Word, and what God perfectly demonstrates in the life of His Son, Jesus Christ. In the life of Jesus, we see that the attributes and qualities of God that are revealed by what Jesus said and did are the supreme representation of what God does, and are therefore both quantitative and qualitative evidence of who He is (Hebrews 1:1–3).

The Bible teaches that God's actions are not random, spontaneous, or erratic. Rather, they are outflows of His nature and essential Being. Therefore, by increasing our knowledge about God, we can correctly relate to God by aligning our thoughts and actions in accordance with what Scripture says that God is like. Additionally, we can best equip ourselves to confidently and competently teach others about the God we have come to know, to trust, and most importantly, to "love with all our heart, all our mind, and all our soul" (Matthew 22:37).

When we fully understand who God is, we will see Him, relate to Him, and love Him as the One True God, the God of Heaven and Earth. We will make Him our Lord and Savior, the one whom we aim to please, and whose will we are desirous of fulfilling during our lifetime.

---

[2] Millard Erickson, *Christian Theology* (Grand Rapids, MI: Baker Academic, 2013), p. 720. The chapter "The Goodness of "God" was instrumental in helping me frame and conceptualize the ideas in the introduction of this book.

Increasing knowledge of God will encourage us to fashion ourselves after the Prophet Samuel, whose response when the Lord called him was, "Speak LORD, for your servant is listening" (1 Samuel 3:10). Samuel did not capitalize on this opportunity to pour out his needs to the Lord by saying, "Listen, LORD, your servant speaks." When we adopt this inverted theology and approach to our relationship to God, we in effect presume to know what is best for our lives and sinfully construct a god onto ourselves. But we must remember, as the Bible so emphatically seeks to teach, that it was God who created us, as opposed to the idolatrous design of a god created after our own fashion and needs.[3]

God created us in His image, and He therefore knows what is best for us in the long run. We will stand before God in the final judgment, not God before us (Romans 14:11). As we increase in the wisdom, knowledge, and revelation of what God does and who He is, we will join with Jesus in proclaiming, "Holy is your name. Your kingdom come, your will be done, on earth as it is in heaven" (Matthew 6:10). I pray that the following twelve Bible lessons contained within this book will educate and inspire you to share your love for God with others and that together we will forge a Christian community in the CrossFit culture by bringing Church into the Box.

YES AND AMEN.

And now… three, two, one, go!

---

[3] William Barclay, *The Acts of the Apostles New Daily Study Guide* (Louisville, KY: Westminster John Knox Press, 1953), p. 155.

In Him –

Greg Amundson

Santa Cruz, CA

LESSON ONE

TURNING WATER INTO WINE

LESSON ONE
TURNING WATER INTO WINE

MY BROTHERS AND MY SISTERS, may the grace of our Lord Jesus Christ, the love of God, and the fellowship of the Holy Spirit, be with you (2 Corinthians 13:14). I want to study with you today the topic of *Turning Water into Wine*. Let's begin our journey together in an environment that many of you are very familiar with: the CrossFit Box®. In the sport of gymnastics, an athlete on the high rings is awarded points based on three factors: risk, originality, and virtuosity. Of these three attributes, the most coveted and illusive is virtuosity— *the ability to do the common uncommonly well.*

These days, I'm more and more impressed and amazed by the greater implications of virtuosity, especially considering that the majority of the things that I do are fairly common to begin with. Let me explain, for I suspect that we are more alike than we are different in this regard.

All through the day, I breathe. Breathing is common. In fact, through the miracle of human creation, God enabled the life-sustaining function of breathing to happen beneath our consciousness and perceptive awareness. It's hardwired into our bodies' automatic nervous system. However, even though it happens automatically—and in this sense it's very common—I can bring my awareness to the next breath that I take, and I can take it with an intention of virtuosity. In other words, I can breath—which is common—uncommonly well.

How about thinking? Have you noticed that you tend to think a lot—or is it just me? Research has demonstrated that the average person has about 60,000 thoughts a day. What's even more interesting (and concerning) is that of these thousands of thoughts, nearly 80 percent are negative, and 95 percent are the same repetitive thoughts as the day before. This leads me to believe that just like breathing, thinking is also among a long list of "common" shared human experiences.

However, just like I can overcome the mundane and common function of breathing, I can direct my awareness to the next thought in my mind, and I can think that particular thought with the intention of virtuosity. In this sense, I can think—which is common—uncommonly well.

Without a far stretch of the imagination, the implications for how much of our life is common is staggering. Unless we are exceedingly careful, our life can become victim to being lived out in a common, routine, average, and predictable way. However, when we remember that we are made in the image of God Himself, then every cell in our body should cry out: VIRTUOSITY!—a hunger and thirst for the uncommon life! Because if there is one thing we very quickly learn about our God, it is that He is uncommon! And as image bearers of God, our life should be uncommon as well.

THE BASICS—WHY WE STUDY THE BIBLE

MY BROTHERS AND MY SISTERS, I propose that we approach our study of God's Word—which for some of us may very well be a common activity—with the spirit of virtuosity. How is this possible?

I propose that there are three steps we can take together to accomplish this goal:

1) Mastery of the Basics: Why the Bible?
2) Knowing the Gospel Message
3) Understanding the Purpose of Jesus Christ's Signs and Miracles

The first reason that we study the Bible is that we believe it is the Word of God. However, we need to be able to conceptualize what this effectually means in our life—and understand it with a level of maturity that empowers us to share our faith with others. This was the expectation of Jesus Himself who encouraged (and commanded) believers to go into the world and to "teach others to obey the commands I have given you" (reference Matthew 28:19–20).

So again, why the Bible?

Let's open the Bible to see what it has to say about itself. In his letter to Timothy, the Apostle Paul wrote, "All Scripture is God *theopneustos*" (2 Timothy 3:16a).

The word choice that Paul settled on to describe and explain the inherent power of the Scripture was a word that he essentially made up! The Greek word *theopneustos* is composed of two other Greek words: *Theo*, which means God or Supreme Being—and *pneó,* which means either wind, spirit, or breath. When we combine these two thoughts into one word, we have the essence of "God Breathed" or "Inspired by God."

However, God did not actually write the words of Scripture. The verse we just read was written by the Apostle Paul, a human being just like you and me. To get a sense of how a human being can write the Word of God, let's turn to the Apostle Peter, who explained it like this:

"No Scripture came about by the prophet's own interpretation of things. For prophecy [or Scripture] never had its origin in the human will [or intellect] but the prophet [or author] though human, spoke from God as they were carried along by the Holy Spirit" (2 Peter 2:20–21—my interpretation within brackets).

So here we have it. God's Spirit—the eternal Third Person of the Trinity— "carried the author along" by empowering them for the purpose of recording God's thoughts onto paper—becoming what we now have the opportunity to study in the form of God's Word.

This means that the Word of God is alive! It's a supernatural book full of power—transformational, life changing, and life-giving power. In theology, we refer to God's Word as *special revelation.* This means that unless and until we open the Bible, we will remain unaware of revelation about God that, at the most fundamental level, *we need to know.* You see, my friends, by implication and definition, revelation means that a person other than the observer needs to take the initiative. In this sense, revelation is God making Himself known to us. And we need to know God!

By way of illustration, when I was in the Drug Enforcement Agency (DEA), I had our nation's highest level of security clearance. I had a need to know matters of national security. It's the same for you, my brothers and sisters—and for everyone under the Sun. The revelation in the Bible is something that we need to know because we need to know God! And most supremely, the Bible reveals to us the nature, image, and exact representation of God in the person of Jesus Christ (Hebrews 1:1–3; Colossians 1:15–19, 2:9).

Jesus Himself said, "I am the way, the truth, and the life. No one comes to the Father except through me" (John 14:6). If we reverse engineer what our Lord said, then until we read the Bible, we will never have an opportunity to receive the revelation of the Gospel message, and we will never know God.

Continuing the thought of Paul, once we know where the Bible *comes from*, we next need to understand *what the Bible does*. Yes—you heard me correctly—the Bible actually does something! How is this possible? Well, the Bible is not your normal book. The same Power that wrote the Book is alive in the Words the book contains. When we receive the Gospel message, supernatural things begin to happen in our life. Look closely at what Paul was describing: "All Scripture is God-breathed and is useful for teaching, rebuking, correcting, and training in righteousness" (2 Timothy 3:16). Let's take an exegetical approach and unpack what Paul meant:

    1) Teaching = God shows me the path;
    2) Rebuking = God shows me where I got off the path;
    3) Correcting = God shows me how I can get back on the path; and
    4) Training = God shows me how I can stay on the path.

Now that we know what the Bible is, and what the Bible does, we need to turn our attention to the One unifying message that the One original Author wants you to know. And in this sense, the Author wants you to Know His Word, and His Word is His Son. This is why the Apostle John wrote that "In the beginning was the Word, and the Word was with God, and the Word was God…. And the Word became flesh" (John 1:1, 14). This means that "the Word is a Person!"

In the spirit of virtuosity—doing the common uncommonly well—let's turn our attention to the heartbeat of the Bible, the Gospel message of Jesus Christ.

UNDERSTANDING THE GOSPEL

IN ACTS 2, THE APOSTLE PETER succinctly and beautifully described a three-step movement that best illustrates the biblical Gospel message. The first movement is the revelation of what God did. Peter declares that Jesus was "a man accredited by God to you by miracles, wonders and signs" (Acts 2:22). Apart from simply being another prophet or religious teacher, Jesus walked the earth in "the fullness of the deity in bodily form" (Colossians 2:9) and was "the radiance of God's glory and the exact representation of His being" (Hebrews 1:3).

Peter's declaration is echoed throughout the New Testament—Jesus was the God-Man to whom all religions point (John. 14:6) and to whom all the prophets testified (Hebrews 1:1–3). Peter explains that according to God's plan and "with the help of wicked people," Jesus was put to death on the cross (Acts 2:23). However, far from being the end of the story, God raised Jesus from the dead in fulfillment of Old Testament prophecy (Acts 2:24–31; cf. Romans 8:11–13) and exalted Him to the right hand of the Father (Acts 2:32–33; cf. Romans 8:34). Finally, Peter addresses the "amazement and astonishment" of the people's response to the pouring of the Holy Spirit onto the faithful believers (Acts 2:12) by announcing that "Jesus received from the Father the promised Holy Spirit and has poured out what you now see and hear" (Acts 2:33).

The second movement of the Gospel involves mankind's response to what God did. Echoing the words of the Jewish converts in Scripture who were "cut to the heart" (Acts 2:37a), humanity cries out in brokenness, despair, and acknowledgment of our need for a savior: "Brothers, what shall we do?" (Acts 2:37b). The result of the Spirit-empowered confession of sin is a fundamental change of heart about who God is. Far greater than a mere change of mind, the new believer's change of heart results in an outward change of behavior that springs from an inward change of desires (1 Samuel 16:7; Proverbs 4:23; Ezekiel 36:26–27). The radical change of heart results in receiving through faith the revealed message about Jesus Christ (Acts 2:41; 2 Corinthians 4:5–6). The objective outward demonstration of faith in Jesus is made visible by baptism and entry into a new community of faithful believers (Acts 2:41; cf. 1 Corinthians 12:12–14).

The final movement of the Gospel involves joyfully receiving what God graciously gives. Through the propitiatory death of Jesus, all who call on His name in faith receive forgiveness of sins (Acts 2:38; cf. Romans 10:13). The subsequent result is the gift of the Holy Spirit and the new life and heart of Christ (2 Corinthians 3:18; cf., Colossians 3:10). The regenerated Spirit-empowered heart is given for the purpose of living a new life as a Christian and participation in the body of Christ (Acts 2:41–47; cf. 1 Corinthians 12:12–27). The Bible teaches that the "heart" often referred to the genuine self as distinguished from appearance, identification with the mind, and physical presence. The "heart-self" had its own nature, character and disposition, which affected the thoughts, words, and actions of the individual. Therefore, a believer whose "heart" is changed through the power of the Holy Spirit will never be the same again (Psalm 51:10; Ezekiel 36:26–27).

The good news of the Gospel is that the savior of mankind has come. In the life, death, and resurrection of Jesus Christ, the faithful believer can be reconciled with God (2 Corinthians 5:11–21; 1 Peter 2:24) and transformed into His image (2 Corinthians 3:18). The promise of the Gospel is that through the process of "putting on the new self" (Colossians 3:10) we will "gradually become brighter and more beautiful as God enters our lives and we become like Him" (2 Corinthians 3:18 MSG; cf. Acts 2:38–47).

WATER INTO WINE

THE APOSTLE JOHN WROTE THAT the purpose of Jesus Christ's signs, wonders, and miracles was "so that you may believe that Jesus is the Messiah, the Son of God, and that by believing you may have life in His name" (John 20:30–31). This is the hermeneutic by which we should interpret every sign, demonstration, and miracle of Jesus. In some way, shape, or form, everything that Jesus said and did was recorded by the Author (upper case "A") so that we could know Him, believe in Him, and have a relationship with Him.

That being the case, let's direct our attention to the wedding feast and Jesus Christ's first miracle. What was Jesus up to? I mean, after all, what we have at first glance is Jesus helping people enjoy their wedding celebration by increasing the amount of wine they can drink. And reflecting on my wilder years on the UC Santa Cruz water polo team, I know firsthand what happens when there is "an increase in wine" at a party. People get drunk! So—again—what was Jesus up to?

The Apostle John was a brilliant theologian. Everything that he wrote in his Gospel and letters contains a rich mosaic of meaning. In the Old Testament, the Prophet Isaiah described the union of God and His people in the context of a wedding celebration. In the 62nd chapter of his prophecy, we find the words, "Indeed, the LORD will delight in you and make your land His spouse. As a young man marries a virgin, your builder will marry you" (Isaiah 62:4). Think for a moment about the magnitude of these words—the One who made the universe—described by Isaiah as "the great builder"—will marry His people. This means that God wants you to participate in His life—and God is eternal. God wants you to participate not just in a human and temporal life on earth, but also in a miraculous way, a divine and eternal life with Him in Heaven.

It's also important that we see the unique biblical view of God presented by Isaiah and all the prophetic voices of Scripture—that God is not some distant deist who winds up the universe and lets it go. The God of the Bible is no "big bang" or blind force, or unified field of consciousness, or cosmic energy. Rather, the God of the Bible is a person who speaks, and acts, and makes an astonishing declaration that He wants to marry His people.

Remember, my brothers and sisters, that Jesus is not just one more prophet in a long lineage of prophets. He is not a spiritual guru or a great teacher. Jesus consistently speaks and acts in the very person of God, and therefore we should not be that surprised that this motif of marriage and wedding comes up in His ministry—in particular, the start of His ministry as recorded by John. In other words, Jesus is in His very person the marriage of divinity and humanity. He's the wedding of Heaven and Earth.

On the other hand, sin is the great divorce—the great chasm of division between God and man. And with the arrival of Jesus, we see the reversal of the pain and anguish of the separation—we are able to see and participate in the reconciliation, the reunion, and the marriage of Heaven and Earth.

Now, what do we see as the narrative unfolds? Jesus's mother is the first to speak in John's telling of the story, and what she says is very direct and to the point. She says, "They have no more wine" (John 2:3).

Remember once again, my friends, that we are reading from the Gospel of John, so we are compelled to approach everything that we read on a number of different levels. On the surface level, Mary is indeed commenting on a social disaster. Running out of wine at a wedding celebration would be embarrassing for the new couple. So on one hand, Mary is asking Jesus to do something very practical. But if that's all she is doing, then we might feel a bit let down, or even worse, to be led to believe that the purpose for a relationship with Jesus is mainly for practical, everyday purposes. In modern speech, it's asking Jesus to do a beer run. So there must be more!

And, of course, there is much, much more. Wine in the Bible is a symbol of exuberance and the intoxication of the divine life. When God is with us, and His Spirit is residing within us, we are lifted up, made joyful, full of life, transfigured, and our minds and our hearts refreshed and renewed. So from this perspective, when Mary says, "they have no more wine," her words are of profound significance. She's speaking at the symbolic and spiritual level about a great lack at the heart of the entire human race. Perhaps some of you today who are reading these words are experiencing the spiritual pain of "having no more wine." In other words, maybe you've run out of the divine life. To a varying degree, the entire human race is experiencing the results of sin, which as depicted in the vivid imagery of our Gospel story, is the result of the great divorce and having "no more wine."

Now, when we see Mary's words within this theological framework, then we can get a sense of the purpose of Jesus's question, "Woman, why do you involve me?" (John 2:4). The implied answer is that Mary is involving Jesus, because the lack of wine has everything to do with Him. In addition, in John's archetypal positioning of Mary, we now understand the greater implications of who Mary becomes in the story. Mary is Eve, the mother of the living—she is the archetypal woman of the Old Testament. As Eve was the mother of the fallen humanity, Mary will become the mother of the renewed humanity.

I think that Mary's next and last line in the Bible is one of the most overlooked and profound verses in the totality of Scripture: "Do whatever He tells you" (John 2:5). On one level, Mary instructs the stewards to do whatever Jesus tells them. However, as we read the story more symbolically, Mary speaks for all the great voices of the Bible—Abraham, Isaac, Jacob, Moses, David, Isaiah, Jeremiah, and Daniel. Mary speaks for the prophets of the Bible who, in more or fewer words, proclaimed, "Do whatever God tells you and you will find life." Think about the implications of Mary's words in your own life as you read the story! Mary is your symbolic, spiritual mother, who says about her Son, our Lord Jesus Christ, "do whatever He tells you."

What Jesus does next is so crucial for us to see and understand. Jesus instructs the servants to fill six stone water jars that were used for ceremonial washing with water. Now, this might seem like a trivial detail.

However, by now, we should be anticipating that there is something more afoot—something very important just underneath the surface. And indeed, my friends, there is.

The jars are evocative of the entire tradition of Jewish religion, tradition, and ritual. In other words, the jars and the "ceremonial washing" are representative of the ways that the Israelites tried to make themselves acceptable to God. Now, on one hand, it's important to see that Jesus is not discounting this. However, what's intriguing is that Jesus now elevates and transfigures it. Jesus wants humans to bring Him all of their power and resources, because Jesus wants to transform, and magnify, and multiply everything we bring Him, precisely so that Jesus can take what we give Him and use it to expand His Kingdom. And when the servants do what Jesus asks, what happens? There are 180 gallons of wine—representative of the essence of the divine life—the wine that never runs out.

As we reach the end of our Gospel story and first Bible lesson, let's pause for a moment and reflect on the purpose of John's Gospel. Everything that John wrote—and remember that everything John wrote was God-breathed—was written so that you would believe that Jesus is the Messiah, the Son of God, and that by believing you would have life in His name.

This being the case, what does the author of this Gospel message have for us today? My brothers and sisters, I propose that God wants you to understand that when you "confess with your mouth that Jesus is Lord, and believe in your heart that God raised Jesus from the dead" (Romans 10:9), you get hooked up to the divine life. In the spirit of today's lesson, you are married to God, and in this sense your life never runs out. When we join ourselves by grace, through faith in Jesus, the celebration of our new life begins.

YES and AMEN.

LESSON TWO

DEVELOPING SPIRITUAL VISION

LESSON TWO
DEVELOPING SPIRITUAL VISION

THE WORD OF GOD:

As Jesus went along, he saw a man blind from birth. His disciples asked him, "Rabbi, who sinned, this man or his parents, that he was born blind?"

"Neither this man nor his parents sinned," said Jesus, "but this happened so that the works of God might be displayed in him. As long as it is day, we must do the works of him who sent me. Night is coming, when no one can work. While I am in the world, I am the light of the world."

After saying this, Jesus spit on the ground, made some mud with the saliva, and put it on the man's eyes. "Go" he told him, "wash in the Pool of Siloam (this word means "Sent").

So the man went and washed, and came home seeing.

His neighbors and those who had formerly seen him begging asked, "Isn't this the same man who used to sit and beg?" Some claimed that he was, while others said, "No, it only looks like him."

But the man himself insisted, "I am the man." The formerly blind man continued to explain; "The man they call Jesus made some mud and put it on my eyes." Then some of the Pharisees turned to the blind man and said, "What have you to say about him?"

The man replied, "He is a prophet." Then a second time the Pharisees summoned the man who had been blind. "Give glory to God by telling the truth."

The man replied, "If this man were not from God, he could do nothing."

Later in the day Jesus found the man and said, "Do you believe in the Son of Man?"

"Who is he, sir?" the man asked. "Tell me so that I may believe in him."

Jesus said, "You have seen him; in fact, he is the one speaking with you."

Then the man said, "Lord, I believe," and he worshiped him.

(John 9:1–7, 8–9, 16–17, 24–33, 35–38)

MY BROTHERS AND MY SISTERS, may the grace of our Lord Jesus Christ, the love of God, and the fellowship of the Holy Spirit, be with you (2 Corinthians 13:14). I want to study with you today the awesome topic of *Developing Spiritual Vision.*

According to the Gospel of Matthew, the very first word that our Lord spoke at the inception of His public ministry was "*metanoeō.*" In context, Jesus said, "*metanoeō* for the Kingdom of Heaven has come near" (Matthew 4:17). The Greek word *metanoeō* means: "To change your mind for the better." In this sense, Jesus said, "Change your mind *for the better*, because I am here." My friends, I am so encouraged by this verse! I believe this verse contains a fundamental principle of the Christian faith that can completely transform your life. Speaking about Himself, Jesus explained that in order to have a relationship with Him, your thoughts about Him would need to change—and they would specifically *need to change for the better.*

In the spirit of radically changing the way we think about God, let's turn our attention to today's magnificent Gospel reading from the Gospel according to John.

In our Bible study today, we come face-to-face with a historical account of Jesus healing a man born blind. The Apostle John explained that all of Jesus's miracles were recorded so that "you may believe that Jesus is the Messiah, the Son of God, and that by believing you may have life in his name" (John 20:31). In this sense, the story of the healing of the man born blind serves the purpose of authenticating the life, ministry, and divinity of Jesus. However, what are the implications of this ancient story for you right here, and right now? In other words, what effect is this story meant to have on your life today? How is an ancient story about a man born blind meant to impact and change you—especially if you can already see?

Let's discover the deeper meaning of this miraculous healing by taking the story one step at a time.

The Bible says, "As Jesus went along, he saw a man blind from birth" (John 9:1). I propose that this is a significant detail in the story because Jesus takes the initiative in healing the blind man. Furthermore, John clues us in to the fact that the blindness has afflicted the man from the moment of his birth. We draw from our Lord's observation of the blind man two conclusions: On one hand, Jesus can see and relate to our suffering. Jesus loves us and wants us to be well. However, it also means something so much more. We are also dealing here with an archetypal story of coming to spiritual vision. Perhaps even more important than healing us physically, Jesus wants to heal us spiritually.

Jesus came into the world to redeem and heal all of humanity—not merely this one isolated individual some 2,000 years ago. In other words, in this particular story, we are all meant to identify with the man born blind. You are the blind man in this story, and Jesus longs to restore your sight. The Bible teaches that we have all been born blind through original sin. This means that humanity suffers from a compromised will and an obscured mind. Simply put, although the eyes in your head might be working just fine, due to the sinful nature of your heart, you still do not see things right, and in this sense you remain blind. Sin blinds us and we are unable to clearly see the deepest truth and reality of the way things are meant to be.

Lest you think I am being cynical or overly negative about the sinful state of human nature, consider the words of the Apostle Paul, who wrote; "Everyone has sinned and we all fall short of the glorious standard of God" (Romans 3:23). And the worst problem of all is that this spiritual blindness and sin have been part of our human nature from the very beginning. We are all born spiritually blind and we don't even know it.

When Jesus observed the suffering blind man, He said, "While I am in the world, I am the light of the world" (John 9:5). This is an astonishing announcement of the divinity of Jesus Christ. As I've said many times in sermons and lectures, Jesus is not just another spiritual teacher, or guru, or even a prophet. Jesus is so much more than this, and in this magnificent self-description, we discover that Jesus is the light by which we see the true nature of God. Jesus is the light that provides you with vision. Jesus is the light by which you safely walk. Jesus teaches you how to see, how to move, and how to act—and this is all conditioned upon Jesus's ability to illuminate the world. My friends, this also implies that without Jesus in your life, you are living in the dark.

Let's turn our attention for a moment to our Gospel author—the Apostle John. In studying the Scriptures, this is an extremely important exegetical detail. By understanding the mind of the original author, we can gain a better understanding of the inspired thoughts within the author's mind at the moment their words were recorded.

What we know for certain about John is that he had an affinity for the Old Testament, in particular, the account of God creating the world. This claim is based on the fact that in the Gospel of John, there is very often a correlation between the life of Jesus and the creation of the universe that we read about in Genesis. For example, John's Gospel begins with the words, "In the beginning" (John 1:1), and this is the same sentence found at the commencement of the entire Bible. John in this sense depicts Jesus as the creative Word of God. And in Genesis, what is the first thing that God creates? According to Genesis, Chapter 1, verse 3, God first created light: "God said, 'Let there be light,' and there was light" (Genesis 1:3). And now we see that the same God who created light in the beginning of the world manifests Himself as the Light of the World in the Person of Jesus Christ.

Throughout the Bible, this is why light is associated with God and the things of God. So in this sense, our Gospel story today is about re-creation, new beginnings, making things new and right, and starting over. The link to creation is then intensified by the next detail we come across. The Gospel story continues and reveals that, "Jesus spat on the ground, made some mud with saliva, and put it on the man's eyes" (John 9:6). This is clearly another connection to Genesis. In Genesis, we read that God fashioned the first human beings from the clay of the earth and then breathed His breath of life into them (Genesis 2:7). In this sense, what we have in the healing of the man born blind is a recapitulation of the creation of the very first human being. John describes for us how the Son of God—the Word became flesh—is going to restore the spiritual life of the man born blind.

This beautiful detail is one of the ways that this story immediately impacts your life today. Jesus is going to restore and complete His creation. This is what Jesus does in your life. He restores and completes you. Now think about this for a moment: If Jesus completes you, this must mean that without Jesus you are incomplete, and in the context of today's Gospel story, without Jesus you are blind.

Friends, let me share with you one of my favorite details about this healing. Notice that Jesus is bringing healing to the man from out of His own substance—

which John illustrates as the "spittle" or "saliva" of Jesus. In the beginning, God created ex nilio—the Latin theological expression for "out of nothing." Creation was achieved through the Word of God, and the Word came forth out of God's own substance. And now Jesus Christ, as the "word became flesh," does the same thing. The spittle of Jesus comes from His own inner life and mixes with the earth. The inner substance of Jesus is then rubbed into the blind man's eyes. In this sense, healing is a result of an immersion into Jesus and His creative power.

What happens next is another wonderful detail in the story. Jesus then tells the man to wash in the pool of Siloam (John 9:7). In the event we overlook or miss the significance of this moment in the healing process, John goes so far as to tell us that the "Pool of Siloam" means, "Sent." Why do you think that John mentions this detail? When we see the "big picture" of John's Gospel, we notice that Jesus continually refers to Himself as the one who has been sent by the Father. In fact, one of the most well-known Bible verses speaks to this very point: "For God so loved the world that *He sent His one and only son*" (John 3:16—my emphasis). Therefore, the Pool of "Sent" is also a symbol of Jesus. The man born blind is now washed in the pool of Christ—a clear indication and reference to baptism. Theologically, baptism is a complete immersion into the life of Christ (reference Romans 6:1–11). This is when the sight is restored: "So the man went and washed, and came home seeing" (John 9:7).

It would be easy to think that the story has reached its pinnacle moment—the man who was born blind can now see. However, what we in fact discover is that the story is just getting started. John wants us to see (no pun intended) that this physical healing is an invitation to spiritual healing. In other words, there is a connection between what is happing physically and what is happening spiritually—and it is the spiritual healing that has the greatest impact on us.

Let's begin by noticing the effect that the healing had upon the friends and family of the blind man—in addition to the formerly blind man himself. When the blind man's friends and neighbors ask: "Isn't this the same man who used to sit and beg?" (John 9:8) there were mixed answers. Some people said, "Yes," while others said "No." What's astonishing is the answer the formally blind man gives when people ask, "Is this the same guy?" With great simplicity the man says, "I am the man" (John 9:9). Now, the English translation here misses a very crucial detail. The man's response in the Greek is *Ego Eimi*, which literally translated into English means "I am" or "I am the one." Once again, when we see this detail within the "big picture" of John's Gospel, the implications are staggering.

The "I Am" phrase is used up and down throughout John's Gospel by Jesus to describe Himself: For example, Jesus says, "I am the bread of life" (John 6:35)—"I am the good shepherd" (John 10:11)—"I am the vine" (John 15:5). And most significantly, just moments before the healing of the blind man took place, Jesus said, "Before Abraham was, I am!" (John 8:58). We notice that once again John is bringing the reader back to the Old Testament.

The "I Am" statements of Jesus—and of the blind man—echo the Old Testament book of Exodus when Moses asked God for His name, and God replied, "I AM WHO I AM" (Exodus 3:14). For our purposes, this means that in addition to his physical healing, the blind man is also experiencing spiritual healing. Having been immersed into the life of Christ, the blind man gains his physical and spiritual vision and is able to see. Through his restored sight, the man is now able to identify with the very life of Jesus. In other words, in addition to having new physical vision, the man has a new spiritual life (reference Romans 6:1–11).

As we progress through the remainder of the story, we are witness to deepening and expanding stages of spiritual vision. This is why the story is relevant for us today. We catch a glimpse of the path of discipleship. We are privy to what happens to our vision and our life as we follow Jesus.

When asked by family and friends the question, "How were your eyes opened" (John 9:10), the man's first response is: "The man they call Jesus made some mud and put it on my eyes" (John 9:11). As we unpack this seemingly insignificant verse, we discover there is so much here. Notice the man initially puts his answer into the realm of what other people profess about Jesus. He says, "The man *they call Jesus*." This is remarkable, because Jesus demands an answer directly from us, not based on what other people think. For example, in the Gospel of Matthew, Jesus first asks his disciples what *other people say* about Him.

After their answer is given, Jesus intensifies the question by asking, "But who do you say I am?" (Matthew 16:15)

This means that Jesus wants a personal relationship with you. Jesus wants each of you to be able to speak from experience about who He is. As we will study throughout this book, this is why faith in Jesus is more than simply following the teaching of Jesus. It's one thing to know about Jesus—it's another thing altogether to actually *know* Jesus.

To this very point, notice what happens next. The Pharisees are mad because Jesus healed on the Sabbath, and they question the blind man about the incident. Remember that the man's first response to the question about Jesus was, "The man they call Jesus." However, here we see something significantly different. When the Pharisees press him with the inquiry, "What have you to say about Him?" The man replies, "He is a prophet" (John 9:17).

Do you notice what's happening here? It started with, "this man Jesus" but then the man's spiritual vision begins to deepen. Now, the answer is more profound and more in alignment with a personal relationship: "This man is a prophet." When the Pharisees argue further the man says, "If this man were not from God He would not be able to do anything" (John 9:33). This answer portrays an even deeper and more profound level of vision. First Jesus was "a man," then "a prophet," and now "Jesus is from God." Having found his physical vision, the man is coming to deeper and deeper levels of spiritual vision.

Now we approach the true pinnacle and climax of the story. Rather than being asked by other people about Jesus, Jesus Himself asks the man: "Do you believe in the son of Man?" to which the formerly blind man says, "Who is he that I may believe in him?" Jesus replies by saying, "You have seen him; in fact he is the one speaking with you now" (John 9:36–37).

This is the moment of the man's complete spiritual–vision restoration. The underlying invitation behind Jesus's question is this: "Are you ready to accept the One?" In other words, Jesus asks, "Are you ready to accept the One who is more than a mere man, more than a mere prophet, more than someone who is from God? Are you ready to accept the One who is God?"

The blind man's response captures the heart of discipleship: "I do believe" the man says, and then he worshipped Jesus. And that's the whole point of the story. Yes, this is an ancient story about physical healing.

But at a deeper level, this is a story about *metanoeō—about changing our mind for the better* and coming to see spiritually who Jesus is. And how do we know that we are seeing Jesus correctly? Much like the formerly blind man, we know that we see clearly when we worship Jesus as Lord and God.

YES and AMEN.

LESSON THREE

A FAITH THAT WORKS

LESSON THREE
A FAITH THAT WORKS

Our first reading takes place just moments before the epic battle of David and Goliath. Due to the fact that David was not enlisted in the Army of Israel, he needed the permission of King Saul to face Goliath in single combat. Let's drop into the scene together to get a better sense of exactly what happened on that historic day.

THE WORD OF GOD:

Saul replied, "You are not able to go out against this Philistine and fight him; you are only a young man, and he has been a warrior from his youth."

But David said to Saul, "Your servant has been keeping his father's sheep. When a lion or bear came and carried off a sheep from the flock, I went after it, struck it and rescued the sheep from its mouth. When it turned on me, I seized it by its hair, struck it and killed it. Your servant has killed both the lion and the bear; this uncircumcised Philistine will be like one of them, because he has defied the armies of the living God."

Saul said to David, "Go, and the LORD be with you."

Then Saul dressed David in his own tunic. He put a coat of armor on him and a bronze helmet on his head. David fastened on his sword over the tunic and tried walking around, because he was not used to them.

"I cannot go in these," David said to Saul, "because I have not tested them." So he took them off.

(1 Samuel 17:33–39)

Our second reading is from the Apostle Paul's letter to the Churches in Rome:

"The night is nearly over; the day is almost here. So let us put aside the deeds of darkness and put on the armor of light … Clothe yourselves with the Lord Jesus Christ, and do not think about how to gratify the desires of your flesh."

(Romans 13:12, 14)

MY BROTHERS AND MY SISTERS, may the grace of our Lord Jesus Christ, the love of God, and the fellowship of the Holy Spirit, be with you (2 Corinthians 13:14). I want to study with you today the topic of *A Faith That Works*.

The more time I spend studying the Old Testament, the more I see that it is full of pictures and images that achieve their greatest portrait of truth in the New Testament. In this sense, although the Old Testament contains biblical history, it also provides a framework for many great theological principles that are more fully developed in the New Testament and life of Jesus Christ. Although the story of David and Goliath may be very familiar to you, in this study, I hope to educate and inspire you to fully understand the magnitude of the spiritual significance that this epic battle contains. Speaking from my own experience in both reading and teaching the story of David and Goliath, we often settle for a very superficial understanding of the story rather then investing in the greater realization that God wants us to achieve. If we think the story is simply a childhood fable about overcoming your giants, then we still have a lot to learn.

Reflect back on the former interpretations of the story of David and Goliath that you have heard about, read about in a book, or seen on TV. If your experiences were anything like mine, you were likely told to "be like David" in an assortment of different ways. Be brave. Believe in yourself. Have confidence in your abilities. Make the most of what you already have. And the most biblically inaccurate interpretation of all: have faith in yourself.

Reaching these conclusions from the text manages to completely miss the point of the story. They instill in us a false sense of hope and tend to focus our attention on the size of our faith, rather than the size of our God. In other words, if we base our chances of victory over Goliath on anything other than God, then it's only a matter of time before our faith falls apart. Allow me to painfully state what should now be obvious: a lot of faith in the wrong thing is a recipe for disaster. However, even faith *the size of a mustard seed*—which is really small—in the right thing (or should we say right Person) is enough to move mountains. That's because it is not the size of our faith that matters. *It's the Size of the One we put our faith in that ultimately makes the difference.*

Here is the main point that I want to make in today's study: if you want to have "A Faith That Works," then you need to take the emphasis off the faith itself and instead focus on the One True God who makes your faith work.

HISTORICAL CONTEXT

THERE ARE TWO OVERLOOKED details of the story that I must bring to your attention. The first is an ancient artifact of biblical era warfare that was referred to as decisive single combat. It was common practice for large armies in the era of King David to select representatives to enter into combat against each other—in these cases, the winner of the match would determine the outcome of the forthcoming battle. This is why in 1 Samuel 17:8–9, Goliath says, "Choose a man to come and fight me. If he is able to fight and kill me, we will become your subjects; but if I overcome him and kill him, you will become our subjects and serve us."

In other words, Goliath was prepared to be the representative of the Philistines, and he wanted the Israelites to select their own representative. The terms of the fight were straightforward: If Goliath won, then the Israelite nation would surrender and serve the people of Philistine. On the other hand, if the representative of the Israelite army won, then the Philistine nation would surrender and serve Israel. This meant that the two opponents that faced each other in one decisive battle would determine the outcome for the lives of the thousands of people that each of them represented. That's a lot of pressure, if you ask me!

There is one other matter of historical significance—the specific location where the battle was taking place. The battle lines had been drawn up in a territory that was already owned and occupied by the nation of Israel—and it was in this place that rightfully belonged to the people of God that Goliath was breathing out defiance and insult.

Although the ancient concept of single decisive combat and the historical locality of the battle may seem like small background details, they are in fact absolutely crucial to understanding key themes that run throughout the entire Bible:

1) As believers in Jesus Christ, the battle has already been won;
2) As believers in Jesus Christ, we live in enemy occupied territory.

In order to have a faith that works, we need to learn how to clearly navigate the battlefield in front of us. This means that we must read the story of David and Goliath both *literally* and *symbolically* in order to apply the spiritual lessons of this great moment in history into our life.

Let's begin with the obvious. Symbolically, who do you think Goliath is in the story? The Scriptures reveal that when Goliath stepped into sight, "All the men of Israel fled from him and were so afraid" (1 Samuel 17:24). Although the people of Israel were in a special covenant relationship with God, the story teaches us that they were held captive in the bondage of fear before Goliath and all that he stood for. This means quite simply that Goliath represents Satan. We know this because biblically speaking, Satan aims to stand against the people of God.

This realization leads us to another startling discovery and a fundamental fact of the Bible. The issue is not about the forces of evil arrayed against the forces of good—rather it is about the devil against God. This means that on the battlefield that fateful day all those thousands of years ago, a decisive battle did in fact take place. What happens to the prince of the powers of darkness—represented by Goliath—happens to all who follow him. And what happens to our Lord—represented by David—happens to all who follow Him.

You see, my brothers and sisters, in this Old Testament story, David represents the New Testament picture of Jesus Christ. However, there is more! On one hand, David is a picture of Jesus Christ who overcame the universal Goliath of sin and death. On the other hand, David is a picture of every child of God who is being made One with Christ through faith and obedience to Him. The Bible teaches that Christ is the Head of His Body. This means that because Jesus achieved victory over the sin and death of Goliath, than through faith in Jesus, so have you.

Through Christ, every battle you ever face during you life has already been won. Are you starting to see the implications of what it means to have "A Faith That Works?" No matter how big the Goliath of your fears may appear to be, the battle is not yours to begin with. In fact, just seconds before David approached Goliath, he said: "The battle belongs to the LORD" (1 Samuel 17:47). This is crucial to understand, remember, and apply in your life. When you catch yourself in a moment of fear, anxiety, uncertainty, or self-doubt, it should be a "red-light warning" that you have put your faith in the wrong thing.

I remember that when I was going through U.S. Army Basic Combat Training, my senior drill instructor said to me, "Everyone wants to be in the Army on a bright, sunny day." Following a dramatic pause he said, "But there aren't any sunny days in the Army!" In my walk with God, I've found that it's the same thing. It's easy to have faith when everything is going well and it's a bright, sunny day outside. However, what happens when your world falls apart and there is hurricane beating down your door? *That's when the size of your faith really doesn't make much difference. What matters is the size of your God.*

I'd like to share with you a few other key details from the story of David and Goliath that direct our attention to Jesus Christ. We have already discovered that David was not in the army. This certainly begs the question—what was David doing on the battlefield? We find our answer in 1 Samuel 17:17. David's father Jesse told David, "Take this roasted grain and loaves of bread to the battlefield for your brothers."

I am immediately awestruck by two incredible New Testament insights into what this means: First, the Scripture teaches us that Jesus Christ Himself is the "bread of life" (John 6:35). The bread that Jesse gave David was to be given to his brothers who were fighting in the battle. Symbolically then, the Old Testament bread that David brought to his brothers becomes the New Testament bread of life that sustains believers in Jesus Christ during every battle we ever face. Second, the Apostle John wrote: "The Father sent the Son to be the Savior of the world" (1 John 4:14). In the same way that David was sent by his father to be the "savior of the day"—Jesus Christ was sent by His Father to be our savior right here, and right now.

OUR IDENTITY IN CHRIST

AS WE APPROACH THE END OF our lesson, I want to bring your attention to one final metaphor from the Old Testament account of David and Goliath. You will recall that King Saul tried to dress David up in his suit of armor. And what was David's response? Although he momentarily donned the armor of Saul, David quickly realized he could not fight in it. The armor did not fit. Specifically, David said, "I have not tested this." This is a significant detail.

David was not about to put his faith in a coat of armor that he had not tested. David's faith rested in God alone.

On the other hand, Saul was convinced that his armor would protect David. Remember, it was after Saul had said to David, "Go, and the LORD be with you" that he dressed up David in his armor. This meant that Saul had the formula—but he lacked the faith.

I really want you to get this point. It's absolutely crucial.

Saul believed in God, that was not the issue. The issue was that despite *believing in God*, Saul still put his faith in his armor. Like most things in the Old Testament, the armor in this case represents more than just a bronze helmet or breastplate. The bronze armor that Saul had put his faith in is distinctly different than the "breastplate of righteousness" that the Apostle Paul speaks about in the New Testament (Ephesians 6:14). Saul's bronze armor symbolizes all our idolatrous attempts to put our faith in something other than God Himself. The bronze armor is our bank account, our jobs, our homes, our health, our fitness, our network of friends, our social status, and our ego. The bronze armor is anything and everything other than God.

So on one hand, we see that David took off the armor that he did not identify with. But that begs the question: Where was David's identity? Clearly, it was in God.

My brothers and sisters—I put this question before you: What does this ancient story have to do with you today?

Before you answer the question, I want to introduce you to another character on the battlefield that day that you might not know about. His name was Jonathan. He was Saul's son—next in line to the throne—and he was a witness to everything that happened during the battle of David and Goliath, and everything leading up to it. Following David's victory, the Bible says, "Jonathan made a covenant with David because he loved him as himself. Jonathan took off the robe he was wearing and gave it to David, along with his tunic, and even his sword, his bow, and his belt" (1 Samuel 18:1–4).

The King James version of this text says, "Jonathan loved David as his own soul." In other words, Jonathan had knit and bound his soul together with David's. Jonathan saw something in David that he wanted in his own life. The fact that Jonathan gave David everything that identified his royal succession to the throne is extremely significant. Jonathan was giving away all of the carnal weapons and associations with Saul in order to cast himself in faith upon David. Jonathan no longer wanted to be identified with his old self. He wanted a new identity.

CONCLUSION

WHAT HAPPENED TO DAVID ON the battlefield that fateful day happened to David's people. David's victory was their victory. The people of Israel who were assembled on the battlefield didn't even need to lift a finger. David did all the work for them. If King David is an Old Testament picture of King Jesus, what does this ancient story mean for believers today? It means that what happened to the King of Kings at the cross in His death, burial, resurrection, and ascension is something that happens to all those who put their faith in Jesus.

In Paul's letter to the Churches in Rome, this is what he referred to when he wrote that believers should "clothe yourself with the Lord Jesus Christ" (Romans 13:14). The believer's identity is now in Jesus Christ—this means the deliberate, conscious Lordship of Jesus over all our desires, motives, and deeds.

Rather than reading the story of David and Goliath and walking away thinking, "I want to be like David," we should in fact pray that through God's grace we could be like Jonathan. Becoming like Jonathan means that we love the Lord Jesus with all our soul, our entire mind, and every bit of our strength. In the spirit of Jonathan, we love Jesus so much that "our soul is knit to His." We love Jesus so much that we lie down at his feet in worship, and we surrender before him every idolatrous item of faith that is in opposition to Him.

Just like Jonathan surrendered his tunic and his robe—representing the artifacts of his ego—we must likewise surrender every aspect of our life to God. When we come to God in faith through Jesus Christ, God will give us new life and new power that we could never achieve on our own. In other words, we win the battle, not according to anything that we do, but according to the victory that Jesus has already won.

YES and AMEN.

LESSON FOUR

STAYING WITH THE LORD

LESSON FOUR
STAYING WITH THE LORD

Our Gospel reading for today's Bible study is from the Gospel according to John.

THE WORD OF GOD:

The next day, John was there again with two of his disciples. When he saw Jesus passing by, he said, "Look, the Lamb of God!" When the two disciples heard him say this, they followed Jesus. Turning around, Jesus saw them following and asked, "What do you want?" They said, "Rabbi" (which means "Teacher"), where are you staying?" "Come," he replied, "and you will see."

So they went and saw where he was staying and spent that day with him. It was about four in the afternoon. Andrew, Simon Peter's brother, was one of the two who heard what John had said and who had followed Jesus.

The first thing Andrew did was find his brother Simon and tell him, "We have found the Messiah" (that is, the Christ). And he brought him to Jesus.

(John 1:35–42)

MY BROTHERS AND MY SISTERS, may the grace of our Lord Jesus Christ, the love of God, and the fellowship of the Holy Spirit, be with you (2 Corinthians 13:14). I want to study with you today the magnificent topic of *Staying with the Lord.*

If you recall from our second Bible lesson, the very first word that our Lord spoke at the inception of His public ministry was "*metanoeō.*" In context, Jesus said, "*Metanoeō* for the Kingdom of Heaven has come near" (Matthew 4:17). The Greek word *metanoeō* means "to change your mind *for the better.*" In this sense, Jesus said, "Change your mind for the better, because I am here." My friends, I am so encouraged by this verse! I believe this verse contains a fundamental principle of the Christian faith that can completely transform your life.

Speaking about Himself, Jesus explained that in order to have a relationship with Him, your thoughts about Him would need to change—and they would specifically *need to change for the better.*

The great theologian and author A.W. Tozer wrote: "The thoughts that come into your mind when you think about God are the most important thing about you." You see, my friends—the thoughts in your mind about God do not change God. The thoughts in your mind about God change you, and they change you for the better or worse, and in direct proportion, to your better or worse thoughts about God. Therefore, of first priority in today's study is adopting two ideas about God that can fundamentally change the way you think about Him as well as the way you think about yourself.

The first thought (or idea) about God that I want you to adopt is this: God knows you better than you know yourself. The second thought about God that I have for you is that He wants you to *stay with Him.*

Let's take these big ideas (or thoughts) one at a time. First things first—the idea that God knows you better than you know yourself. In order to understand what this big idea means, we need to go back in time: 2,000 years back in time!

In biblical-era Palestine, ox yokes were made of wood. In application, a farmer brought his ox to a carpenter to begin the process of measurement taking and a careful study of the animal's disposition, characteristics, strengths, and unique tendencies. The yoke was then meticulously constructed so that it would fit well and not hurt the neck of the animal. In other words, each yoke was handmade with love and a great deal of care so that it would perfectly fit and support the ox.

During a Bible study with my dear friend and pastoral-mentor Chaplain Richard Johnson, he shared with me an ancient legend that Jesus, himself a carpenter, fabricated the finest ox yokes in all of Galilee, and that men from all over the country came to him to buy the best yokes that human hands could make (refer to the William Barclay NT Bible commentary on Matthew, Chapter 11).

Similar to our business practices today, shops had signs above their door in biblical times. In Messianic–Rabbinic verbal tradition, it is said that the sign above the door of our Lord's carpenter shop in Nazareth read: "My yokes fit well." Although this ancient story is not from Scripture, we should certainly take note that Jesus often referred to Himself as a yoke. For example, in the

Gospel of Matthew, Jesus said to his disciples, "Take my yoke upon you and learn from me, for I am gentle and humble in heart, and you will find rest for your souls, for my yoke is easy, and my burden is light" (Matthew 11:29–30).

In my daily walk with Jesus, I have happily discovered that He tailor makes for me a "yoke" of exactly what I need at the exact time I need it. In other words, it's as if Jesus whispers in my heart: "Let me tailor make for you what you need to go through life." How can Jesus possibly "tailor make for me what I need?" Well, of course He can! God created me—He knit me together in my mother's womb; He knows the sound of my voice; He's counted every hair on my head—which is all to say that He knows me better than I know myself. My brothers and sisters—it is the same for you. God knows you. God loves you. God sees you and He knows the sound of your voice. And God wants to have a relationship with you, which leads us to our next big idea. You see, my friends, the first big idea is about God loving you. The second big idea deals entirely with your response to God's gracious love.

The second big idea about God that I want to share with you is that He wants you to *stay with Him*. To understand the significance of what this means in your life, let's turn our attention to our Gospel reading, and the awesome exchange between Jesus and His disciples.

To begin, we must understand and appreciate the brilliant mind of our Gospel author, the Apostle John. A literary master, John wrote his Gospel and epistles in such a way that he designed sacred word-pictures that are meant to reflect and portray our relationship with God. The scene that we read in our Gospel took place in the vicinity of the Jordan River, where John the Baptist was baptizing. John is standing with two of his disciples and observes Jesus walk by (John 1:36). Without hesitation, he tells his followers, "Behold the lamb of God" (John 1:36).

My friends, let's not kid ourselves about what John the Baptist said. There is something terrifying in this description. John is telling his disciples that Jesus is the one who will be sacrificed for the sins of the world. The "lamb of God" is not a gentle and meek image. In fact, it's quite the contrary. As the lambs were brought into the temple to be slaughtered for the sins of the people, Jesus would be put to death for the sins of the world.

So who were these two disciples with John? For our purposes today, these two figures become immediately important. These two disciples are a symbolic, spiritual, and archetypal reflection of you. So who are they? The two men with John were youthful people—maybe 18 or 19 years old—and a fine example of the spiritual seekers of their time. They were young people filled with spiritual enthusiasm and passion for meaning, purpose, and mission in life. This is what had brought them to John the Baptist in the first place. Now do you understand why you are meant to identity with these two disciples? These two young people are trying to figure life out—just like you are! These disciples are a reflection and image of you trying to figure it all out and find the secret to life. And so, when their great mentor says, "There is the lamb of God," they drop everything and go after him. Keep in mind that these two young people were Jews, so they knew exactly what John meant by Jesus being the "Lamb of God." But nevertheless, they followed after Him.

This is such a beautiful detail of the spiritual life. We need to have the courage to follow Jesus even when it does not make perfect sense. Even when we don't know exactly where we are going, we still need to follow after Him. Even when what He says goes against the grain of what we want to do—we still need to listen, follow, and obey.

The Bible speaks a great deal about the human quest for God. And we see it here, in the way these two young people run and follow after Jesus. However, the Bible is not primarily about our quest for God. *It's about God's quest for us.* And we are able to see it here in John's Gospel picture. The two young men initially come running after the Lord. However, notice what happens next. Jesus turns on them and asks them a question (John 1:37–38).

In the traditional discipleship path of other world religions, it is the devotees who ask the guru questions about life. But here, we see something entirely different. We see God asking the question. And what a question it is! Jesus asks, "What do you want?" (John 1:38). Let that sink in for a few moments. Allow this to be a point of meditation for the remainder of your life. And even right now, in this very moment that you read these words—allow this profound question to sink deeply into your heart. Imagine that our Lord is right in front of you, and He turns and asks you, "What do you want? What are you seeking?"

What would you say in that moment? That is why this question is so important! What would you say? It's interesting that very often in life, we do have a sense of what we want. However, after you get what you want, have you noticed that you want something else, or more of what you already received? Or perhaps you no longer want what you had toiled so long and hard to get! In the context of profession, material wealth, relationship, and education—we know the answer to these questions.

But the Lord brings the question from the head to the heart. And because it's a question of the heart, it's unlikely that you would respond to Jesus by saying "Lord, I want more money, more pleasure, more success." Something in your heart would give you a gentle nudge and say, "This is definitely not the right answer." We know at a place deep within us that these things do not give us the joy we are looking for. That being the case, would you ask for contentment, peace, joy, meaning, mission, or purpose in life? After all, these desires seem to be more "spiritual" and in alignment with the path of discipleship.

Well, perhaps. After all, these are certainly legitimate answers. But listen to how the disciples respond. It's a great question from Jesus, and it's going to be a great question from the disciples! The disciples answer the Lord's question with a question of their own: "Rabbi, where are you staying?" (John 1:38).

How interesting to answer a question with a question—not to mention the seemingly childlike quality of the question. To ask where Jesus is staying? Couldn't these two guys come up with a better question? Here is the Lord of the universe asking, "What do you want? What are you looking for?" And they ask, "Where are you staying?"

But I propose their instincts were in fact completely right. Just a few moments before this scene took place, we read one of the most important verses in the entire Bible: "The Word became flesh and dwelt among us" (John 1:14). What does this mean? The "Word," or *Logos* in Greek, speaks to the creative power and mind of God. And here is the main point that John makes about the Word of God. God's Word—His nature, power, and mind—became flesh. This means that God's Word does not remain something abstract and distant, something you have to go off and search for or read about. "God's Word became flesh and *dwelt among us.*" God's Word became a person whom we can see, and touch, and talk to. In fact, this is exactly what the Apostle John explained about Jesus in his first epistle: "We offer you the word of life. The word that our eyes have seen, that we have looked upon, that our hands have touched" (1 John 1).

There is the entire story of the Bible in a single verse—the entire message of the Christian faith in one line of Scripture. The word became flesh, a person, whom we can have a relationship with. And that is why the instinct of the disciples in this scene is so good. They know the answer to the deepest longings and desires of their heart are to stay with Jesus. In other words, what they are searching for is not going to be found in a book, or spiritual laws, or new sets of ideas. Nor was it going to be found by walking a particular religious path. It was to be found in the person of Jesus Christ—and by staying in fellowship with Him.

This detail of the story reminds me of the first time I met Londale Theus. I was a brand new deputy sheriff in Santa Cruz County. In the roll-call room, I noticed a flyer advertising a "Knife Defense Course for Law Enforcement" offered by the Santa Clara County Sheriff's Office. The course topic sounded intriguing, and the following week I drove to a small martial arts dojo near Hayward to experience the training firsthand. Within just moments of meeting the course instructor, Londale Theus, I knew that I had found a man I wanted to follow. Londale was the first American law enforcement officer to become a certified Krav Maga Black Belt with the prestigious Krav Maga Association of America. He had served as a sergeant on the Santa Monica Police Department SWAT Team and had a commanding presence that I had never seen before (and have not since). So what did I do following the course? I followed Londale! For the next eight years, I spent as much time with him as possible. In other words, I did everything I could to *stay with him*. This means that the lessons of the dojo were secondary to the lessons of life that Londale was imparting to me.

This remains a key feature of discipleship and in our relationship with Jesus. In fact, this is exactly what we read about in the Book of Acts. In describing what happened when John and Peter went on trial before the Sanhedrin, Luke wrote that, "When they saw the courage of Peter and John and realized that they were unschooled, ordinary men, they were astonished and they took note that these men had *been with Jesus* (Acts 4:13—my emphasis). It was not about books, or about laws, or commands, or lessons. What set John and Peter apart was the fact that they had been with Jesus. *They had stayed with Him.* And Jesus had completely transformed their life.

Here is another great detail from our Gospel reading. John tells us that is was 4PM. Nothing is incidental in John. Just like every brushstroke of a master painter is important, every detail that John writes is significant. We hear that Jesus died at 3PM (Mark 15:33). Therefore, spiritually, the 4PM time designates and speaks to what comes after the Cross. It designates the time of the resurrection. This means that these two disciples who come and stay with Jesus at 4PM are evocative of all of us who want to stay with the Lord. Why is this the case? Because Jesus Himself said, "Very truly I tell you, it is good for you that I am going away. Unless I go away, the Advocate will not come to you; but if I go, I will send Him to you" (John 16:7). In other words, when Jesus was on the earth, His presence was limited to His physical locality. In order for the disciples to *stay with Jesus*, they needed to be physically in His presence. However, for the followers of Christ after His ascension to the Father, we now experience personal fellowship with Him, through the Holy Spirit, every moment of our life.

So how do you stay with Jesus and experience the fellowship of the Holy Spirit? Daily prayer. Meditation. Fellowship with other believers in the Body of Christ. Reading from the Word of God. Attending Church, ministry gatherings, and Bible studies, just like you are doing right now. These are all ways of staying with the Lord and welcoming the Spirit of God into our life.

It is at this point in our Gospel story that we discover the name of one of the disciples. Andrew is the brother of Simon (Peter). The first thing that Andrew does upon leaving the presence of Jesus is to tell his brother about the person he had met. "We found the Messiah!" (John 1:40–41). Notice the enthusiasm and passion for evangelism! And it wasn't that Andrew simply told his brother about Jesus. He did more than that. The Bible says that Andrew *brought his brother* to Jesus. I am so inspired by Andrew's heart for evangelism.

When you see a great movie, you want to tell people about it. When I found Krav Maga and CrossFit, I wanted to share them with everyone. In fact, they are what inspired me to open my CrossFit and Krav Maga studio in Santa Cruz! It seems to be built into our psyche—when we find something beautiful that we love, we want to share our good fortune with others. And that's what happened here. Once the disciples stayed with Jesus, they wanted to share what they had found with their family and friends.

And notice the person whom Andrew brought to Jesus. It was none other than Peter, the "rock" that Jesus would build His Church upon. It was Peter, who would be the chief of the Apostles. It was Peter, the apostle who would become the focal point of the Church. It was Peter, who would walk on water! And without Andrew and his heart for evangelism, then Peter would have never come to Christ.

This is our call to action. We all know someone like Peter. Each one of you knows someone whom you should bring to Christ. Do you think that Andrew could have imagined the power and magnitude of what his introduction to Jesus would result in for Peter? This leads me to believe that we never know the long-term effects that our Gospel-centered words of encouragement and love will have in the lives of other people. And lest you think that you are not gifted enough to preach the Gospel, take comfort in these words of Saint Francis of Assisi: "Preach the Gospel at all times. When necessary, use words." In application within your life, this means that just like Peter and John, people should look at you and think: "This person has been with Jesus."

And so here we have it, my brothers and sisters. God loves you. In fact, He loves you so much that He asks you, "What do you want?"

And how you answer this question might just change your life.

YES and AMEN.

LESSON FIVE

SITTING AT THE FEET OF JESUS CHRIST

LESSON FIVE
SITTING AT THE FEET OF JESUS CHRIST

THE WORD OF GOD:

As Jesus and His disciples were on their way, He came to a village where a woman named Martha opened her home to Him. She had a sister called Mary, who sat at the Lord's feet listening to what He said. But Martha was distracted by all the preparations that had to be made. She came to Him and asked, "Lord, don't you care that my sister has left me to do all the work by myself? Tell her to help me!"

"Martha, Martha," the Lord answered, "you are worried and upset about many things, but few things are needed—or indeed only one. Mary has chosen what is better, and it will not be taken away from her."

(Luke 10:38–41)

MY BROTHERS AND MY SISTERS, I come bearing the *euangelion* of the Bible—the Gospel of Jesus Christ. The Greek word *euangelion* means "good tidings" or "good news." The promise of the Gospel is that when Jesus Christ enters your life, your life will gradually become brighter and more beautiful as God transform you into the image of His son and you become more like Him (2 Corinthians 3:18—my interpretation).

This means that when you put your faith in Jesus, God begins the process of changing you from the inside out. In some cases, the transformation is immediate—in other cases, the process is more gradual. However, one thing is always certain: when the Spirit of God Himself dwells within you (1 Corinthians 6:19), your world is turned upside down. You begin to realize that you have new priorities. New values. New mission. New purpose. New desires. New heart. New life. The people who have known you for years are going to be astonished.

In our Bible study today, we will be seeking the answer to two critical questions that have resounding implications for our daily walk with Jesus. The first question deals with affirming the deity of Jesus Christ. Once we understand *who Jesus Christ is*, we are then prepared to ask our second question—How we can become more like Him? The answers to these profound questions have an astonishing impact on your life.

THE DEITY OF CHRIST

THE MOST CRUCIAL TOPIC IN CHRISTIAN discussion today is the deity of Jesus Christ. In theological studies, the doctrine of Christ's deity is referred to as Christology, and it sits at the very heart of the Christian faith. What sets a disciple of Jesus apart from a disciple of Lord Buddha, Lord Krishna, Lao Tzu, or any other spiritual teacher from the various world religions, is the believer's grace-empowered profession of faith that God walked the earth in human flesh in the person of Jesus Christ (John 1:1, 14; Colossians 1:15–19, 2:9; Hebrews 1:1–3).

You really need to hear this astonishing biblical claim in the fullness of what it means: Jesus was not just some extraordinary person—not even the most extraordinary person who has ever lived. Although I would certainly not argue against the fact that Jesus was indeed the greatest and most extraordinary human being the world has ever known, I contend that we cannot stop with the greatness of Jesus Christ's *humanity*. Rather, we must turn our attention to Jesus Christ's *deity*. The Christian faith rests on Jesus actually being God in human flesh (Colossians 2:9).

There are several reasons why this is important—for the purposes of our study today, I will focus on what I feel are the two most significant. The first is that Jesus allows mankind to have real knowledge of a transcendent God. Jesus said, "Anyone who has seen me has seen the Father" (John 14:9). Whereas in the past, there were many prophets who spoke the Word of God, in the person of Jesus, we now have God Himself speaking (Hebrews 1:1–3). This is why the Apostle John wrote: "In the beginning was the Word, and the Word was with God, and the Word was God ... and the Word became flesh" (John 1:1, 14). This is crucial for us to understand. What instills Jesus Christ's words, teaching, and demonstrations with such power, significance, and authority over our life? It's the fact that Jesus is God! The author of Hebrews explained it like this: "Going through a long line of prophets, God has been addressing our ancestors in different ways for centuries. Recently, God spoke to us directly through His Son" (Hebrews 1:1–2 MSG).

Here is a practical way to strengthen your understanding of this verse: there was a time in human history when prophets told mankind *information about God*. However, in the incarnation, humanity now has the awesome opportunity not just to be told *about God*—now we can actually *know God*. Even more astonishing is the fact that believer's are indwelt by the Spirit of God Himself (Romans 6:10–11). Listen to these words from the Apostle John to really drive home the power of what this all means: "That which was from the beginning, which we have heard, which we have seen with our own eyes, which we have looked at and our hands have touched—this we proclaim concerning the Word of Life" (1 John 1:1). Notice the descriptive words that John used: John *heard Jesus—saw Him* with his own eyes—*touched Jesus* with his own hands. That is remarkable because it means that for John, it was not theoretical *head knowledge about God*. John had actually experienced a relationship with God Himself.

Now, what do John's words, written two thousand years ago, have to do with you today? We needn't guess, because John plainly tells us: "So that you can experience it right along with us" (1 John 1:3). Notice John's use of the word *experience*. John wants you to have the same *experience of God* that he did! Not read about. Not talk about. Not be told about. John makes the radical claim that believer's can actually *experience* Jesus—and therefore God—in a real, tangible, and life-changing way.

The second reason Jesus Christ's deity is significant is that it compels us to *worship Him*. Jesus is not just another great spiritual teacher in a long lineage of spiritual teachers. He is not a guru. He is not a self-help master or someone who we can have a casual Sunday-school day of communion with. Because Jesus is in the *same sense* and to the *same degree* as God Himself—then Jesus equally deserves the praise, adoration, obedience, and worship that we give to God. This means that although we have many love relationships in our life, we need to love Jesus supremely, uniquely, and in a way that is unlike any other relationship we have ever known. As our Gospel story will help us understand, we need to relate to Jesus in such a way that He is the *one thing necessary*.

EXPERIENCING GOD

OUR STUDY THUS FAR HAS resulted in substantiating the biblical witness to the deity of Jesus Christ. In theological terms, the biblical witness of Jesus Christ is referred to as *special revelation*—in other words, revelation is God's own self-disclosure of truth about Himself that we would not be able to discern through any other means. Through His Word contained within the pages of the Bible, God showcases (or "represents," according to Hebrews 1:3) His nature uniquely and supremely in the person of Jesus Christ.

As important and significant as biblical revelation is, it is equally important to understand that it is only one side of the coin. This is due to the fact that revelation has the potential to result in *information* absent any *transformation*. In addition to learning about what God does, we must also pay attention to *what we do in response to what God reveals*. Borrowing from the incredible insight of C. S. Lewis: "It is Christ Himself, not the Bible, who is the true Word of God. The Bible, read in the right spirit … will bring us to Him."

This being the case, the question becomes: What is our response? How do we respond to the deity of Jesus? To answer the question, we turn to the words of Jesus Christ Himself: "Love the Lord your God with all your heart, and with all your soul, and with all your mind" (Matthew 22:37). With the great commandment of Jesus Christ as the basis for how we respond to God, let's revisit our Gospel story to help us understand how we take the *information* we have in our mind about Jesus and *move it into our heart*.

MARTHA AND MARY

OVER THE AGES, THERE HAVE been three main interpretations of the account of Jesus at the home of Martha and Mary. The first centered on the active lifestyle demonstrated by Martha, in contrast to the contemplative lifestyle demonstrated by Mary. The second interpretation focused on the priority of the spiritual life witnessed by Mary, as opposed to the distractions of the world that consumed Martha. It's interesting to note that the popular secular and business principle of focusing on *The One Thing* indirectly borrows from this interpretation of the Gospel story.

Finally, many scholars have emphasized an interpretation of the story that focused on Christ's concern for the needs of outcasts and less fortunate members of society. During biblical times, it was common for men to gather around the feet of a rabbi to receive instruction. This was the traditional locality for men, whereas women would be relegated to such tasks as preparing food and tending to other housekeeping matters. Needless to say, Mary seated at the feet of Jesus, in the company of a room full of men, ran against the socially normative practices of the time.

Although I find these three different interpretations of the story compelling, very recently, the Holy Spirit opened my eyes to yet a fourth way of understanding the Gospel account. In light of the theme of our study, *I propose that Mary and Martha could symbolically be seen as the same person experiencing two different states of consciousness.* In this sense, we are reading an ancient story about our current state of being—this makes the story immediately relevant to our daily life. Therefore, the tension between Martha's concern for the *many things* and Mary's concern for the one thing that *matters most* represent the struggle that takes place within our mind as we attempt to discern the priority of the different thoughts that consume our attention.

In other words, what we could call the fourth model of interpretation builds on the historical understanding of the duality between the active and contemplative lifestyle. The traditional view and interpretation of the early Church Fathers was their focus on the superiority of the contemplative life—in the story of Martha and Mary, this is represented in the tension between action and contemplation. Although Martha (representing action) asks Jesus to tell Mary (representing contemplation) to help her, Jesus does not allow it. Mary and Martha are sisters with distinct gifts, and they are meant to live together in harmony. Nevertheless, Jesus seems to suggest that Mary, representing contemplation, has greater access to the presence of what matters most—God Himself in the person of Jesus Christ. This is why Jesus says, "Mary has chosen what is better, and it will not be taken from her" (Luke 10:42).

Something very similar happens in the Gospel of John and the account of the resurrection of Lazarus (John 11:1–45). In this story, Martha and Mary (the sisters of Lazarus) represent two different levels of spiritual understanding—what we will define as *head knowledge* and *heart knowledge*.

Martha represents *head knowledge*—however, she may not fully understand all that she is saying or even thinking. Despite the fact that her brother Lazarus has been dead four days, she declares: "Lord, if you had been here, my brother would not have died. But even now I know that God will give you whatever you ask of Him" (John 11:22).

Martha clearly has great intellectual understanding about what Jesus is theoretically capable of. She thinks that if Jesus had arrived earlier, her brother would not have died. In her mind, she also thinks that Jesus has the ear of God, and that even now there might be something that Jesus can do, although it is not specified what that might be. In this sense, her mental posture is one of activity—she grasps the doctrine, but misses the person. This means that although our mind might be filled with ideas about God, our hearts could still remain far from Him. Martha soon leaves the scene, returns home, and tells her sister Mary, "The Teacher is here, and He is asking for you" (John 11:28).

Even the title that Martha uses in referring to Jesus—a teacher—seems to suggest her overemphasis on intellect, and less on heart. Martha now hands over the conversation to Mary and, in doing so, it is important to take notice that the transition happens in secret. This means that the shift in consciousness is not immediately available for others to see, because it occurs in the hidden depths of the believer, symbolized by Mary's posture at the feet of Jesus in the Gospel of Luke. In addition, it is important to see that Jesus calls for Mary. Whenever Jesus calls someone, it is for the purpose of participating in the fullness of His life. Although Martha went out to meet Jesus on her own—perhaps suggesting on her own terms—Mary is called by name, the way a good shepherd calls his sheep. Mary responds to Jesus according to the terms that He has established.

This means that in Mary, the believer is witness to something that we are called to model as we respond to who Jesus Christ says He is. In alignment with our interpretative key of Mary and Martha symbolically representing the same person in two different states of consciousness, we see the great chasm of difference between knowledge of the head and the wisdom of the heart. The Scripture tells us: "When Mary reached the place where Jesus was and saw Him, she fell at His feet and said, 'Lord, if you had been here, my brother would not have died'" (John 11:32).

Does this verse sound familiar? It should! That's the exact same thing that Martha said only moments earlier. However, notice the change of posture—physical, spiritual, and mental. Mary is at the Lord's feet, with the same posture we see her adopt in the Gospel story of Luke. Her confession of faith is not just a matter of reciting doctrinal truth about Jesus. Rather, Mary's faith in Jesus has moved from her head into her heart. The intimacy of Mary and Jesus in the scene is witnessed in their mutual weeping over the death of Lazarus—a key detail that was missing in the interaction with Martha.

AT THE FEET OF JESUS

RETURNING TO THE STORY OF Jesus at the home of Martha and Mary, we now have a most powerful means by which we can enter into the presence of Jesus and worship Him as Lord and God. As we seek to model the behavior of Mary and sit at the feet of Jesus, we must understand that we are not choosing between two different characters—and thus two different lifestyles—the active and the contemplative. Rather, we are distinguishing between two different states of our own consciousness. On one hand, the Gospel story reveals the importance of physically removing ourselves from those things that "worry and upset us." On the other hand, the story also reveals how easy it can be to relocate our physical body to one place, while our thinking is left behind—painfully consumed with what worries and upsets us.

How do we embrace both the physical and mental posture of Mary and learn to "sit at the feet of Jesus, listening to what He says" (Luke 10:39)? I propose that sitting at the feet of Jesus means that we enter into His presence, and this is achieved through the practice of meditative prayer. However, we must distinguish between prayer as the activity of an already busy mind, and rather see it in the context of a disciplined and regenerated heart.

For many people, prayer means nothing more than the mental activity of speaking to God. We use the same "voice in our head" that we use at every other moment throughout the day. Even if we "speak to God" through the recital of memorized verses of Scripture, the tendency of our consciousness is to use the same faculty of our mind that we use to recite any other information that we have committed to memory.

But notice in the Gospel story that Mary is not talking—she is listening. In addition, the physical posture of her body—seated at the feet of the Lord—implies a posture of rest, submission, and worship. In this sense, it is both a physical, mental, and spiritual posture.

Prayer of the heart is distinctly different than prayer of the mind, and for our purposes, will be referred to as biblical meditation. In humility, I offer this definition: *Biblical meditation is sitting in the presence of God with our mind in our heart.* To borrow from the imagery of the account of Jesus at the home of Mary and Martha—it is that point of our being where there are no divisions or distractions—we are no longer worried or upset about the many things—we have come to rest in the presence of the One who matters most. Mary teaches us that the presence of God dwells in our heart, and it is here that the great encounter with our Lord can take place. It is here that *heart speaks to heart*—it was this encounter of two hearts becoming one that resulted in such profound intimacy that Mary and Jesus wept together.

It is imperative that we understand the way the word "heart" is used in its full biblical meaning. In the Bible, the heart is the seat of human will: thus, the heart is the central and unifying organ of our personal life. Our heart is the place where God dwells and is therefore the ideal place of prayer. To pray with our heart means that we direct our consciousness to God from the center of our innermost being.

THE PRAYER OF THE HEART

WE NOW TURN OUR ATTENTION to the means by which we can pray with our heart. In other words, we discern the biblical path to meditation. There is a general framework to meditation that should be understood more as characteristics rather than hard and fast rules:

1) The prayer of the heart is nurtured by short, simple prayers;
2) The prayer of the heart is repetitive; and
3) The prayer of the heart carries no judgment or expectation.

In my meditative prayer life and walk with our Lord, I have found great comfort in the fact that it was one simple phrase on the tax collector's lips that was enough to win the mercy of God (Luke 18:9–14); it was one faithful and humble request of a thief on a cross that resulted in eternal life (Luke 23:42–43); and it was Mary's tears at the feet of Jesus that captured and moved His heart.

Following a slow and deep breath through the nostrils, the silent repetition of the ancient prayer—"Lord Jesus Christ, Son of God, have mercy on me"— can help you descend with your mind into your heart.[4] If it is more agreeable to you, a word or short verse from Scripture repeated silently with your eyes closed can achieve the same affect. In both instances, the prayer of the heart can help you concentrate and create an inner stillness and thus listen to the voice of God. On the contrary, if you sit still, close your eyes, and try to force your mind to be silent, it often results in the opposite effect—you find yourself bombarded by thoughts and ideas, and in the context of our Gospel story, you become consumed by many things that "worry and upset you." However, when you use a simple phrase such as "Lord Jesus Christ, Son of God, have mercy on me" or other verse from Scripture, it is easier to let the many distractions of life pass by without being misled, ensnared, or consumed by them. The simple and repetitive prayer of the heart can slowly empty out your crowded interior life and create a quiet space where you can dwell with God.[5]

The prayer of the heart contains one additional principle—it should take place without judgment, and without expectation. In other words, when you close your eyes and begin to repeat your prayer, do so in the spirit of Mary at the feet of Jesus. No agenda. No plans. No anticipated feelings or outcome. No expectations. And if you should notice that you are thinking a thought other than your prayer, notice that thought without judgment. Simply recognize the departure from your prayer—and then quietly and gently return to the prayer itself.

---

[4] The *Prayer of the Heart* was first brought to my attention in the masterful book *Into the Silent Land* by Martin Laird and by subsequent spiritual discipleship with Father Kevin Joyce.

[5] Henri Nouwen, *The Way of the Heart* (New York, NY: Ballantine Books, 1981), p. 74.

The beauty of the prayer of the heart (what we now refer to as biblical meditation) is that if you are faithful to the prayer and practice at regular times each morning, the prayer will open your awareness to God's active presence throughout the remainder of your day. For example, when you sit quietly with your eyes closed in the morning and repeat, "The Lord is my shepherd" (Psalm 31:1a), the Scripture takes up residence within your heart and remains embedded there throughout the day. Even while you navigate the hustle and bustle of your day, the prayer continues to maintain a steady pulsation within your heart and keeps you attuned to God's active presence in your life. In this sense, through the power of the Holy Spirit, the prayer continues to "pray itself" within you even while you fully participate in the demands of your daily life.[6]

There is one final characteristic of the prayer that serves as both a blessing for your life and the lives of all the people who God has entrusted to you. When you take your prayer, and move from your mind into your heart, you bring with you into the presence of God all the other mental preoccupations that were of concern to you before you started praying. Those concerns or thoughts in your mind that are offensive to God's Holy nature are purified from your consciousness (Psalm 51:10; 139:23–24). On the other hand, when you descend from your mind into your heart with loving thoughts of other people, then all those who have "been on your mind" are also led into the healing presence of God.

The prayer of the heart is how your individual prayer life can enrich your walk with the Lord and enable you to become more like Him. Furthermore, the prayer of the heart can be a ministry and blessing to your family, your friends, your loved ones—and the entire world. In other words, the prayer of the heart is one way that you can "Love the Lord with all your heart, with all your soul, and with all your mind—and love others as yourself" (Matthew 22:37–39).

YES and AMEN.

---

[6] I am indebted to Henri M. Nouwen and his book The *Way of the Heart* for helping me frame and conceptualize this section on *praying with the heart.*

LESSON SIX

GETTING CLOSE TO THE FIRE

LESSON SIX
GETTING CLOSE TO THE FIRE

THE WORD OF GOD:

When it was almost time for the Jewish Passover, Jesus went up to Jerusalem. In the temple courts he found men selling cattle, sheep and doves, and others sitting at tables exchanging money. So he made a whip out of cords, and drove all from the temple area, both sheep and cattle; he scattered the coins of the moneychangers and overturned their tables. To those who sold doves he said, "Get these out of here! Stop turning my Father's house into a market." His disciples remembered that it was written, "Zeal for your house will consume me."
(John 2:13–17)

When they saw the courage of Peter and John and realized they were unschooled, ordinary men, they were astonished and they took note that these men had been with Jesus.
(Acts 4:13)

That which was from the beginning, which we have heard, which we have seen with our own eyes, which we have looked at and our hands have touched—this we proclaim concerning the Word of Life.
(1 John 1:1)

MY BROTHERS AND MY SISTERS, may the grace of our Lord Jesus Christ, the love of God, and the fellowship of the Holy Spirit, be with you (2 Corinthians 13:14). I want to study with you today the topic of *Getting Close to the Fire*. Whenever we open the Word of God, we do so with the intention of "increasing in wisdom, stature and favor with God and Mankind" (Luke 2:52). To this extent, we study the *words* of Scripture. As important and valuable as this pursuit is, we need to continually remind ourselves of the miraculous truth that these words proclaim: "The Word became flesh" (John 1:14). This means that *until* and *unless* our study of Scripture leads us into the fire of a personal, loving, and saving relationship with the Word—God Himself in the Person of Jesus Christ—then the words we read in the Bible could just as easily be the words we read on our social media feed.

Before we move into an exegetical survey of our Gospel readings, I'd like to begin with two complementary illustrations—one true story from my life, and the other imaginary—to help provide context for our study. The purpose of framing our Bible study in this fashion is to really drill down and understand the difference between reading from the Word of God—and having a relationship with the Word of God Himself.

AN ILLUSTRATION FROM MY LIFE

WHEN I WAS SERVING AS a special agent in the DEA, I attended a 30-day assessment and selection course to test for a position on the Forward Advisory Support Team (FAST)—the federal government's equivalent of a domestic SWAT team. The course was held in Quantico, Virginia, during the winter of 2010. My previous assignment was on a Border Enforcement Security Taskforce on the southwest border of Calexico and Mexicali. Needless to say, I was far more accustomed and acclimated to the desert heat than the frigid East coast winters.

Part of the training, assessment, and selection included survival training in which candidates were taught how to make a field-expedient fire. In the classroom, I gained "head knowledge" about the dangers of hypothermia and the steps to mitigate the harmful effects of prolonged ice and snow exposure. Twenty-four hours later, all the head knowledge about fires, warmth, and gradually reheating the body did me absolutely no good—I didn't need theory, I needed application!

During a land navigation exercise, I'd slipped while climbing on a branch over a freezing-cold, fast-moving river and had fallen in—completely submerging myself. I had only a few minutes to reheat my body's core temperature or I was going to be in serious trouble. What I needed was a fire—not just "head knowledge" about the benefits of a fire in the context of a hypothermic episode.

I needed the real thing! Thankfully, I was able to make the fire; draw near to it; and gradually reheat my body, my gear, and my uniform.

Put yourself in my situation. Imagine you are freezing cold and have a book in your hand that describes all different types of fires: small fires, big fires, fireplace fires, bonfires, woodland fires, commercial fires, beach fires, gas-stove fires—the list goes on and on. If you're minutes away from freezing to death, will the words in the book describing the varying degrees of heat produced by the different types of fires suffice to save your life? Or do you want to actually experience the heat that the words in the book are describing?

Very well, then. Now imagine that you are freezing cold and off in the distance see a well-lit fire. You are close enough to see the fire—perhaps even hear the sound of the crackling wood—but you are still too far away for the heat of the fire to effectually provide you with any warmth. What do you do? Well it's common sense—you draw near to the fire. And because you are so cold, you want to do more than simply draw near or walk by. You want to sit down and warm yourself by the fire.

THE DESERT FATHER TRADITION

NOW LET'S PRESS THIS ILLUSTRATION into a beautiful story from the Desert Father tradition. I was introduced to the Desert Fathers in my first year of seminary studies at Western Theological Seminary. The Fathers were ascetic monks who lived in the Egyptian desert during the 4th and 5th centuries. When Church persecution ended, these monks had escaped into the desert as a way of following Jesus and escaping the temptation of conformity to the world. The Fathers found inspiration in St. Paul's exhortation: "Do not model yourselves on the behavior of the world around you, but let your behavior change, modeled by your new mind. This is the only way to discover the will of God and know what is good, what it is that God wants, and what is the perfect thing to do" (Romans 12:2—New Jerusalem Bible).

And now, our story from the desert.

THREE YOUNG MEN USED TO GO and visit blessed Father Anthony every year. Two of the young men would discuss their thoughts and the salvation of their souls with him, but the third always remained silent and did not ask him anything. After a long time, Father Anthony said to him: "You often come here to see me, but you never ask me anything," to which the young man replied, "It is enough to see you, Father."

———————

Pause for a moment and reflect on your daily routine. If your days are anything like mine, then you are a very busy person. We have meetings to attend, many visits to make, many people to see. Even if our social life were temporarily put on hold during the recent shelter in place—the life of our *social media* kept plugging away, perhaps at an even more rapid pace than before. Our calendars are filled with appointments, our days and weeks filled with engagements, our years filled with plans and projects. We are pulled in so many different directions, with so many seemingly conflicting priorities, that we tend to be at the mercy of social compulsions—which ultimately results in very compulsive behavior.

I think *compulsive* is really the best term here. I know it's a harsh and accusatory term when we apply it to ourselves—but sometimes we need a wake-up call in order to produce radical change in our life. *Compulsion* points to mankind's ongoing and increasing need for affirmation. We ask ourselves, "Who am I?" And our answer is, "I'm the one who is liked, praised, admired, loved, disliked, hated, despised." Whatever your profession or role in society, what tends to matter is the way that you are perceived by others. If being busy is perceived by others as being a good thing—then you need to be busy. If having money is perceived by others as a good thing—then you must earn more money, and cling to the money you already have. If knowing lots of people is perceived by others as a good thing—then you will have to make more contacts. In other words, the compulsion manifests itself in the lurking fear of failing and the steady urge to prevent this failure by accumulating more of the same—more work, more money, more friends.

Compulsive thinking and behavior are the result of the two main enemies of the spiritual life: anger and greed. These destructive tendencies of our ego prevent us from obtaining loving relationship with ourselves, with each other, and—most importantly—with God. Reflecting on our first Gospel story, anger and greed are evocative of the livestock drivers and money marketers who take up residence within the sacred Temple Courts.

And here we must momentarily pause to prayerfully contemplate the words of the Apostle John: "The light shines in the darkness, and the darkness has not overcome it" (John 1:5). John, of course, in his use of the word "light" is referring to Jesus Christ. When we feel surrounded by darkness—the sinister feelings of anger, pride, greed, anxiety, fear, jealously, insecurity—no amount of theoretical head knowledge or self-help guru gibberish is going to work. We need to draw near to the Light—the Fire—the Word become flesh—Jesus Christ.

Within this framework and context, let's review and examine our second and third Gospel readings:

SECOND GOSPEL READING

When they saw the courage of Peter and John and realized they were unschooled, ordinary men, they were astonished and they took note that these men had been with Jesus.

(Acts 4:13)

THIRD GOSPEL READING

That which was from the beginning, which we have heard, which we have seen with our own eyes, which we have looked at and our hands have touched—this we proclaim concerning the Word of Life.

(1 John 1:1)

WHAT WAS IT ABOUT PETER and John that had the Pharisees shaking in their sandals? There was something about these two guys that was both *astonishing* and *captivating.* They couldn't take their eyes off of them. These were a couple of nobodies: no formal education, no wealth, no social contacts, no Instagram followers, and no Facebook account. So what was it about Peter and John that astonished the Pharisees? It was the fact that they had *been with Jesus.* Rather than reading about the fire, or observing the fire from a distance,

Peter and John had been at the fire's side for three years. In this sense, they had set themselves on fire!

The Pharisees were astonished because they were beholding two guys who had been set on fire by God Himself. The fruit of the Spirit—love, joy, peace, forbearance, kindness, goodness, faithfulness, gentleness, and self-control (Galatians 5:22–23)—these gifts of the Spirit are not manifested by *reading about them in a book.* They happen as a result of the Spirit of God Himself taking up residence within you. The fire burns inside of you, and the heat of your life blesses others. In other words, your life is a ministry. People see Christ in you. The Message translation of the Bible describes it like this: "We are transfigured much like the Messiah, our lives gradually becoming brighter and more beautiful as God enters our lives and we become like him" (2 Corinthians 3:18 MSG).

The Apostle John describes something similar in his first Epistle (our third Gospel reading). Notice how John describes his relationship with Jesus—seeing Jesus, hearing His voice, touching His hands. It was not about doctrine, theology, laws, regulations, or rituals. It was about cultivating a relationship with Jesus. And how was the relationship cultivated, fostered, developed, and maintained? By spending time with Jesus.

My brothers and sisters, I propose that what we need *now more than ever* is to spend time—in silence and in solitude—with Jesus. To use the beautifully descriptive mandate of the Bible: "You need to sit alone in silence, for the LORD has put it upon your heart" (Lamentations 3:28). No agenda. No plans. No wordy prayers. No music. No journal. No headspace app. Just you and Jesus sitting still before God's mighty throne of grace. This is how we pick up His heat—how we warm ourselves—how we restore and refresh ourselves and recalibrate our mind and our heart. And what should we expect to happen when we spend time with Jesus? Speaking from experience—sometimes when Jesus comes into our life, he comes with a whip! He overturns what we think is important, and He reestablishes order.

JESUS AT THE TEMPLE COURTS

THE APOSTLE JOHN'S STORY OF Jesus clearing the temple is a wonderful testimony of how people who are spiritually asleep, blind, deaf, and mute (not to mention dead) do not actually look that way *on the outside.* However, no matter how grandiose our outward appearance may appear to be, it always pales in comparison to the inward disposition of our heart (1 Samuel 16:7). At the temple courts, for all intents and purposes, the people appeared to be engaged, energetic, and even keenly entrepreneurial—strategically positioned within the temple itself; the cattle yard and money market meant that those who came to *pray* first had to *pay.* Jesus's sharp rebuke, "Stop turning my Father's house into a market!" (John 2:16), seems to suggest His general dissatisfaction with the human tendency to desecrate what God makes Holy and sets apart for His purposes.

When Jesus enters the temple, His purpose is to reestablish order. To turn the temple back into the place it was meant to be—a place of worship. Now keep that image in your mind for a moment—Jesus entering the temple, driving out everything that is impure, reestablishing order, putting first things first—keep this in mind as you consider the remarkable words of the Apostle Paul: "Don't you know that your body is a temple of the Holy Spirit?" (1 Corinthians 6:19). What Paul was explaining to the Churches in Corinth was that the true dwelling place of God was no longer in the temple in Jerusalem. Now the temple is in the very bodies of the followers of Jesus. Did you hear that? As a disciple of Jesus, your body is the place where God dwells.

Jesus described it like this: "Whoever has my commands (my Words) and keeps them (lives by my Word) is the one who loves me. The one who loves me will be loved by my Father, and I too will love them and will manifest myself to them. Anyone who loves me will obey my teaching (my Words). My Father will love them, and we will come to them and make our home in them" (John 14:21–23—my interpretation within the parentheses).

I think these words of Jesus are what led Paul to explain to the Churches in Rome that believers should "Make their body a living sacrifice" (Romans 12:1). The backdrop of Paul's remarkable statement must be understood in the context of Old Testament sacrificial rituals of temple purification. The purpose of the sacrifice was that humans were signaling their desire to be one with God—the sacrifices were meant to accomplish the unity of Divinity and humanity. And now Paul exhorts the Churches in Rome that disciples of Jesus need to purify themselves! Why? Because as believers in Jesus Christ, our body is now the place where the unity of Divinity and humanity are meant to come together.

Now that we are warmed up, let's make this real. When we bring the "body-temple" insight of Paul alongside the image of Jesus clearing out the Temple Court together—we have ourselves a radical hermeneutic by which we can understand our Gospel story. If your body is meant to be a temple where God is praised, that means that every aspect of your life needs to be turned over to the Lord—everything needs to be dedicated to Him—everything needs to be a sweet offering—a sacrifice onto the Lord. Your mind. Your will. Your heart. Your body. Your business. Your friendships. Your exercise. Your entertainment. Everything in you is meant to be a living sacrifice of praise onto the Lord.

PRACTICAL APPLICATION

MY BROTHERS AND MY SISTERS—what would happen if you allowed Jesus with that whip of cords to enter into the temple of your body—what would happen? That's the purpose of the story! It's not something intriguing that Jesus did long ago. It's something He wants to do right now. Today. Maybe even in this very moment! I'll be the first to admit that it takes immense humility and courage—but as disciples of Jesus, we need to let Jesus loose in our life. We need to allow Him to knock some things over.

Did you notice the mess He made in the temple that stirred everybody up? That's going to be very similar to the mess He makes in us when we allow Him into our life to cleanse, purify, and reestablish order. This means that whatever in you that is not utterly dedicated to God needs to be transformed—turned over—and given to Him. The great theologian Abraham Kuyper put it like this: "There is not one square inch in the whole domain of our human existence over which Christ, who is Sovereign over all, does not cry out: 'Mine!'"

In the spirit of our illustration—sometimes it gets hot by the fire! But the heat is good for us. It purifies us. The implications for one of the most frequently referenced Proverbs in the warrior tradition are immense: "As iron sharpens iron, so one person sharpens another" (Proverbs 27:17). The heat and fire of the furnace is the context for the hammering and forging process the Author speaks to in this verse. Who is this Person who wants to come into our life to sharpen us? God Himself, in the person of Jesus Christ.

So now we have it, my friends. We need to spend time every day with Jesus. But how do we know we are in His presence, and that His presence is with us? Well, coming back to our Gospel story—we should expect that some pieces of our life are going to get turned upside down! Suddenly you notice that you have new priorities. New values. New mission. New purpose. New heart. New life. The very people who have known you for years are going to be astonished.

YES and AMEN.

LESSON SEVEN

SALT AND LIGHT

LESSON SEVEN
SALT AND LIGHT

Our Gospel reading for today's lesson is from the Gospel according to Matthew.

THE WORD OF GOD:

Jesus said, "You are the salt of the earth. But if the salt loses its saltiness, how can it be made salty again? It is no longer good for anything, except to be thrown out and trampled underfoot. You are the light of the world. A city built on a hill cannot be hidden. Neither do people light a lamp and put it under a bowl. Instead they put it on its stand, and it gives light to everyone in the house. In the same way, let your light shine before others, that they may see your good deeds and glorify your Father in heaven."

(Matthew 5:13–16)

MY BROTHERS AND MY SISTERS, may the grace of our Lord Jesus Christ, the love of God, and the fellowship of the Holy Spirit, be with you (2 Corinthians 13:14). I want to study with you today the topic of *Salt and Light*. My goal in today's study is to provide you with inspiration and education on the concept of your *personal identity*. Now, you might be thinking to yourself—*I already know who I am*. Reasoning from this fact, take a few moments to reflect on *who you think you are*. How do you describe yourself—to yourself? Here are a few prompt's to help you get started:

What are your greatest attributes?

What are your strengths as a person?

What are the character traits you are most proud of?

Now that you're all warmed up, consider this question—how much of your daily thinking do you allocate to thinking about the thoughts you have about yourself? Where do these thoughts come from? Are they even true? To what do they owe their source? Are they serving your greater good or are they a downward spiral of self-destruction? And most importantly, is the person who you *think you are* consistent with the person who *God says you are*?

Lest we remain under the assumption that positive self-talk and self-affirming personal descriptions are a function of modern psychology, we need to remember that the very first set of complementary questions ever asked of mankind—in other words, the first question that appears in the Bible—had to do with human identity and *who we think we are*. In the creation account of Genesis, God asked Adam the question: "Where are you?" (Genesis 3:9). The complementary set of parallel questions, "Where are you?" (Genesis 3:9), and "Who told you that you were naked?" (Genesis 3:11), speak to the physical and metaphysical nature of human identity. Our "location" treats humanity's physical posture in our relationship to God, whereas our "nakedness" speaks to our guilt and total depravity.

Now reflect back on those character traits and self-descriptive attributes that you came up with a few moments ago. Perhaps you described yourself as strong, handsome, and well spoken. Or, maybe you thought that you were weak, ugly, and tongue-tied. But in either case, the theological question that you should really be asking yourself is this: "Who told you that you were strong, handsome, well spoken, weak, ugly, or tongue-tied?" In this sense, the basis for the question that God asked Adam is now the basis for the question that God asks you: "Who told you that you are who you think you are?"

You see, my friends, as our Creator, God has exclusively reserved for Himself the right to elaborate, define, describe, and detail the person who you are. God does not want anyone else—including you—to tell you who you are. God wants to do it Himself.

Why would this be the case? Well, in the context of the question that God asked Adam, the answer becomes immediately clear. Adam did not know that he was naked until someone else told him that he was naked. Now, you might be asking yourself, "what's the big deal with nakedness" The biblical and theological idea of nakedness represents shame—and shame was not an idea organic or original to Adam's mind. Rather, someone else (Satan) impregnated the idea of shame into Adam's mind.

So again, let's return to this question of your identity. Who do you think you are? How convinced are you that the person who you think you are is the person who you really are? Let's take this a step further: How certain are you that the person who you think you are is the same person who God says that you are? Now that's the million-dollar question!

Before we go any further, I want to be clear on something: I certainly have no intention of speaking against positive self-talk. I actually think it's very important. In fact, for years, I traveled around the world teaching the CrossFit Goal Setting and Positive Self-Talk Course. I instructed thousands of people on the benefits of developing a positive mental attitude and maintaining a healthy sense of personal identity. However, here is something I realized in all those years of teaching: no matter how grandiose someone's sense of self-worth was—I have never met anyone who described himself or herself as *salt, light,* or *a city set on a hill.*

A NEW SENSE OF SELF

IN OUR GOSPEL READING FOR today's lesson, Jesus compares His disciples to three things—*salt, light, and a city set on a hill.*

As we begin a close exegetical reading of Mathew 5:13–16, notice that all three of the descriptive characteristics that Jesus speaks to—*salt, light,* and *a city set on a hill*—do not exist for themselves. Rather, all three exist for something or someone else.

Salt. I feel very confident in writing that you did not describe yourself as being *salt.* Am I right? However, if Jesus is describing you as *salt,* then there must be something about salt that is absolutely essential for you to understand and relate to. Therefore, let's start with salt and the historical context of this now common and readily available household-cooking item.

In Jesus's time, salt was used to season and preserve meat. Keep in mind this was 2,000 years ago—eons before the idea of electricity or a refrigerator had even been conceived of. In the times that we now live, we can simply put our steak and chicken into the refrigerator to keep them from going bad. However, in biblical times, meat had to be cured in order to preserve it and prevent it from spoiling. And the curing agent that was relied upon to this effect was salt.

Although the predominant purpose of salt during biblical times was to preserve food—in this sense to maintain the *fertility of food*—it was also used for the exact opposite effect: to render the earth *infertile.* For example, when a conquering nation wanted to utterly eliminate an enemy city, they would tear down its walls, burn all of its buildings to the ground, and then, in a final and decisive act of total destruction, salt the earth. The process of salting the earth would ensure that nothing would ever grow there again. So salt in this sense serves two purposes: salt can preserve, and salt can destroy.

Notice in both instances that salt was not used itself. In other words, salt is not valuable itself—rather salt is valuable in *what it does* and *how it affects* other things.

By the same token, light is not for itself. Rather, light allows us to see things by it. Light ensures that we are walking on the right path and not getting lost in the dark. Light illuminates things upon which it shines. Most importantly, light is a quality and descriptive characteristic that the Bible uses for Jesus Christ. For example, the Apostle John speaks to the fact that Jesus Christ is the "light of all mankind" and the "light that shines in the darkness." John described Jesus as the "true light that gives light to everyone else" (Reference John 1:4–9) and the author of Hebrews described Jesus as the "radiance (sunlight) of God's glory" (Hebrews 1:1–3).

Remember that Jesus—as the very embodiment and perfect example of everything that light should be—did not come into the world for Himself (reference John 3:16). The purpose of Jesus Christ's light was to benefit others. In this sense, we can now understand that in the context of *salt* and *light,* in both instances, Jesus is implying that they are qualities and attributes about *who you are* that are meant to *benefit other people.*

With *salt* and *light* out of the way, let's turn our attention to a city set on a hill. At first reading, we are faced with the strange idea that somehow and someway we are meant to relate to ourselves as a city: but not just any city. Specifically, Jesus tells us that we are a *city set on a hill.* What did Jesus mean by this? Much like describing yourself as *salt* (very unlikely) or *light* (well, perhaps), it is unlikely that you have ever described yourself as a *city set on a hill.*

However, think back to the beginning of our study. The thoughts that you believe about yourself are only valuable to the degree that they are in alignment with what God says about you. And God plain as day tells you that you are a *city set on a hill*! In fact, this is exactly how Jesus both sees you and describes you. So in this sense, just like *salt* and *light*, we have a hermeneutical clue:

there must be something about a *city set on a hill* that benefits other people. And indeed there is!

In ancient times, a *city on a hill* was a point of navigation. Travelers walking across a vast and open desert-land would make their way through the wilderness by navigating according to a *city set on a hill*. In other words, a *city set on a hill* was like a compass. And because this particular city was set on a hill, it could be seen far off in the distance. In another navigational context, a city set on a hill might be compared to a lighthouse used by maritime captains to safely travel across the vast and open ocean. Furthermore, a *city set on a hill* would be a refuge for travelers and a safe place for them to take shelter, seek restoration, and find refreshment from endless days in the desert.

SELF-SERVING OR BLESSING OTHERS

THINK BACK ONCE AGAIN TO the way that you described yourself at the beginning of our study. It's interesting to note that when we describe ourselves—our attributes, qualities, and unique gifts—we tend to focus on the qualities that benefit us. However, the way that Jesus sees you and describes you has more to do with your relations to the world around you rather than with your relations to yourself. Remember, Jesus describes you as *salt, light,* and a *city set on a hill*. In this sense, what matters most to God is that you matter most to other people.

In the same way that Jesus brought light into the world, through His Spirit within you, you can bring His light into the world with everything that you say and do. In the same way that Jesus enhances, sustains, and saves your life—as salt, you are called to enhance, sustain, and share the good news of the One who came to save the world. In the same way that Jesus is the "city on a hill that all nations flood to" (reference Isaiah 2:1–3) you are called to be a city by which other people can see what is good, and just, and right. In other words, all of the unique and special gifts that God gave you—including the fact that you are *salt, light,* and a *city set on a hill,* are not meant for yourself. They are meant for others.

MISSION AND PURPOSE IN LIFE

THIS ALSO MEANS THAT YOU find mission, purpose, and fulfillment in your life to the degree that you bring God's love to others. As followers of Jesus, you are meant to be *salt*. Being *salt* effectively means that you preserve and enhance what is best in society around you. On the other hand, you are *salt* in the sense that you undermine and confront what is evil, unjust, dysfunctional, and sinful in the surrounding culture.

This might be a radical notion for some of you. Have you ever thought of your life in the way that God describes you? Have you ever considered your mission and purpose in life as being *salt*, or *light* or a *city set on a hill*? Well, according to God's Word—to preserve, highlight, season, illuminate, set apart, and position on high all that is best in God's Kingdom is exactly what you are called to do. By implication, this also means that whether it is through prayer, lawful social action, or service in the warrior professions, as *salt* you are also called to confront the injustices and evils of the world.

God also describes you as *light*. This means that you are *light* to the degree that people around you are able to see what is worth seeing. You help illuminate the right path for other people. You shine light into darkness. You bring hope and brightness into people's lives.

God is calling you to be a beautiful, just, holy person—*a light*—and by the integrity and brightness of your light, you can shed light around you. You illuminate what is beautiful and, by the same token, help people see what is unhealthy, sinful, and out of alignment with the will of God.

In other words, by the very integrity of your life, you will highlight what is good in society—and contrast it with what is dysfunctional. The clear implication of being *salt, light*, and a *city set on a hill,* is that you make the world a much better place! You help people see what is good. You illuminate the right path. People can navigate their life based on the example you set. People look at your life and think, "Oh, that's what we are meant to be. That is what God wants."

In the event you have not thought of yourself along these lines, I want you to read this once again. I want this Truth of God's Word to move from your head right down into your heart.

Through the Power of God's Holy Spirit…

You are the city by which people can navigate their lives.

You are the light by which people can clearly see.

You are the salt that adds seasoning, flavor, and joy to life!

My brothers and my sisters—to this I say:

YES and AMEN.

LESSON EIGHT

THE WORK OF LOVE

LESSON EIGHT
THE WORK OF LOVE

THE WORD OF GOD:

Jesus said, "For the kingdom of heaven is like a landowner who went out early in the morning to hire workers for his vineyard. He agreed to pay them a denarius for the day and sent them into his vineyard.

"About nine in the morning he went out and saw others standing in the marketplace doing nothing. He told them, 'You also go and work in my vineyard, and I will pay you whatever is right.' So they went.

"He went out again about noon and about three in the afternoon and did the same thing. About five in the afternoon he went out and found still others standing around. He asked them, 'Why have you been standing here all day long doing nothing?'

"'Because no one has hired us,' they answered.

"He said to them, 'You also go and work in my vineyard.'"

(Matthew 20:1–7)

MY BROTHERS AND MY SISTERS, may the grace of our Lord Jesus Christ, the love of God, and the fellowship of the Holy Spirit, be with you (2 Corinthians 13:14). I want to study with you today the topic of *The Work of Love*. Humanity has much to learn about the divine origins of our creation. After having been seemingly lost for several days, Jesus's parents found the young boy inside the temple. Deeply distressed, Mary said to Him, "Son, why have you treated us like this? Your father and I have been anxiously searching for you" (Luke 2:48). Gazing into His parents eyes, Jesus replied "Didn't you know I had to be in my Father's house?" (Luke 2:49). Has anything changed for mankind today? We are akin to Joseph and Mary as we anxiously search for the One Person who provides meaning in our life and the proper context for a relationship with each other. And all the while the essence of Jesus's words reverberates through the Universe: we must learn to see the "Father's house" as a reflection of the locality within human nature where God Himself longs to dwell.

SOCIAL STATUS AND POSTURE

THERE SEEMS TO BE A DRIVE within human nature to strive for social status. Theologically speaking, posturing with extravagant outward religious acts of prayer, almsgiving, and fasting are practiced because people "want to be seen" (Matthew 6:1–18). Mankind's outer emphasis on social esteem (How many likes? Are my followers increasing? Did that post get a comment?) prevents us from attending to the spiritual vitality of the sacred interior space of the heart. The pollution and contamination of our temple-body prevents contact with our "Father who sees in secret." Vigorous effort for notoriety in the social order of things—*often expressed in the social media of things*—tends to blunt spiritual maturity and proper discernment between the many things and the *One thing that matters most* (Luke 10:41–42).

Recent events in the United States are harsh evidence of what happens when social preoccupation takes a particularly dark turn in an effort to either maintain or disrupt economic and civil arrangements. The Bible has much to say on these matters. In fact, the Gospel often presents the people on top of the social ladder as obsessed with their position and willing to do anything to keep it: Gentile leaders are sharply rebuked because they "lord their position" over others instead of leading by example and helping those in need (Matthew 20:25; 1 Peter 5:3); the rich man who wears fine apparel and feasts on gourmet food easily ignores the nearly naked and starving beggar at his gate (Luke 16:19–31); astute leaders put heavy burdens on others without lifting a finger to actually help them (Matthew 23:4); and as the tension of our Gospel story will reveal, men can plan to stone only one party in a two-act crime in order to trap a prophet (John 8:3–6).

The Bible reveals that when people become overly consumed with rules, laws, and regulations that govern the relationship between human beings, it becomes woefully easy to completely dismiss the spiritual dimension of life. Quite simply, idolizing the law takes time and energy. Most importantly, when law becomes god, mankind becomes derailed, distracted, and ignorant to the Maker of the Moral Law Himself.

THE MORAL LAW

THERE APPEARS TO BE a unifying feature of moral life. An abiding hunger and thirst for something more—for an eternal reality that transcends the fleeting beauty of the world. There is *something within our nature* that points us toward *something beyond our nature*. The Bible puts it like this: "God put eternity in our hearts" (Ecclesiastes 3:11). It is a desire for something more—but a "more" that is distinctly apart from anything that we can satisfy by our own efforts. This desire was certainly being expressed in the life of the rich man as he ran toward Jesus. The Bible tells us that he is rich—this means that he had accomplished many great things of the world—yet he still hungered for something more.

"What good thing must I do to inherit eternal life?" (Matthew 19:16).

We see here the fundamental expression of Mosaic faith—the association between doing something and achieving something in return. Although an ancient religious tradition, it nevertheless begs the question: Has anything changed for us today? We are hardwired for eternity—to seek something more—but at the same time humanity seems to have a self-imposed governor within our mind that equates a *particular amount work* with a *particular amount of reward*. At the socioeconomic level, this is played out in the principle of a fair hourly wage— working an hour to receive in return an hour's worth of wages. However, this is a function of the limitations of mankind's mind—not of God's Kingdom. In fact, Jesus turns this worldly principle completely upside down in the parable of the *Workers in the Vineyard* (Matthew 20:1–16).

THE PARABLE OF THE VINEYARD

WE BEGIN BY NOTING THAT SEVERAL workers were hired at different times of the day—all of them on the agreement of receiving a denarius (the usual daily wage of a day laborer) for a full day's work. The landowner went out early in the morning—likely before sunrise—then again at 9AM, 12PM, 3PM, and 5PM, each time enjoining workers to come and work in his vineyard.

At the end of the day, the landowner told the foreman to call the workers and pay them for their wages, beginning with the last ones hired and going on to the first (Matthew 20:8). The workers who were hired at 5PM came and received a denarius, and the same amount was paid to the workers hired at 3PM, 12PM, and 9AM.

Well, friends, what do you think the workers who were hired before sunrise—the first laborers to be employed by the foreman—expected to be paid? After all, they were hired first, which means they worked the longest. Economically speaking, they worked more hours then the workers hired at 9AM, 12PM, 3PM, and most certainly the workers hired at 5PM—thus it would seem to follow in their reasoning that because they had the privilege and honor of working the entire day, they were entitled to (and should expect) a greater reward for the *greater amount of time, effort, toil, and work* they had expended.

The Scripture teaches that this was indeed their expectation: when those who were hired first came to the foreman to be paid, they *expected* to receive more. But each of them also received a denarius. When they received it, they *began to grumble* against the landowner. "These who were hired last only *worked for one hour*, yet you made them equal to us who have borne the burden of *working all day* in the heat of the sun" (Matthew 20:12—my emphasis).

It follows from this parable that mankind is hardwired to expect to be either rewarded or punished for what we do or fail to do. But can you see how this mindset and predisposition is antagonistic to the Grace of God? God always gives us what we do not deserve, what we cannot even begin to work for, and what we cannot achieve on our own. This is the Gospel message of Grace. Paul says it best: "For it is by grace you have been saved, through faith—and this is not from yourselves, it is the gift of God—not by works, so that no one can boast" (Ephesians 2:8–9).

THE RICH MAN

IN OUR GOSPEL READING TODAY we are privy to a front row seat in the arena of the tension between work—effort, toil, labor, "good deeds"—and the Grace of Jesus Christ. So what happens? How does Jesus answer the question of the rich man when he asks, "What do I need to do?"

First, we must notice and admire the fact that the rich man comes to Jesus—in fact he runs—to God Himself—to find the answer to the burning question in his heart: *How do I find what matters most?* He is seeking the good that can only come from Jesus—the only person in whom any sense of Ultimate Good can be found. Notice therefore the posture in which this places the rich man. The rich man is in the passive rather than the active. He is ready to listen to what God says. And what does God say?

Jesus responds, "If you want to inherit life, keep the commandments" (Matthew 20:17). What our hearts need to see in this verse is the relationship and interplay between *Jesus Himself* and the *commands to which Jesus speaks.* Where else in the Scripture does Jesus speak on the principle of obedience to the Commands of God? This question lands us squarely within our theology of Christology. As fully God and fully man (Hebrews 1:1–3; Colossians 2:9), Jesus points to Himself as the One to whom we are called to obey. For example:

1) "If you love me, obey my commands" (John 14:15).
2) "Anyone who loves me will obey my teaching" (John 14:23).
3) "Anyone who does not love me will not obey my teaching" (John 14:24).
4) "If you keep my commands, you will remain in my love" (John 15:10).
5) "You are my friends if you do what I command" (John 15:14).

What we discover is that according to Jesus, the teaching and Teacher are inseparable. We love, obey, follow, listen to, and surrender to a Person—God Himself—not a collection of crafty philosophical or spiritual doctrines. This is why at the reinstatement of Peter, Jesus asked him three times "Do you love me?" (John 21:15–19). Never once did Jesus ask Peter, "Do you love my teaching? Do you love my lessons?" No. Jesus wanted a loving relationship with Peter. Jesus knew that everything else would flow perfectly from that.

Jesus tells the rich man to follow the commandments. However, it is interesting to note that the commandments that Jesus speaks to are from what is historically referred to as "the Second Tablet." Jesus enumerates and puts in first position those commandments that have a negative form—"You *shall not* murder, *you shall not* commit adultery, you *shall not steal*, you *shall not* give false testimony" (Matthew 19:18).

This means that if you want to live in friendship with God—if you want fellowship and entry into the life of discipleship with Jesus Christ—then it seems to follow that there are certain things you have to remove from your life. In other words, if there are things in your life that are egregious to God—then you have to cut them out. So in this sense it's interesting to note that the "work" of the commandments that Jesus points to depicts what we are *not to do rather than what we are to do*. Expressed another way, this remarkable verse teaches us that *sometimes in the spiritual life what we refrain from doing is equal if not more important to what we effectually (or actually; in fact) do.*

AN EXAMPLE FROM THE BOX

LET'S PRESS THIS INTO a context that many of you are familiar with. Imagine that you are a CrossFit Box owner who greets an enthusiastic potential new client at the threshold of the doors to your studio. This person asks you in a matter-of-fact fashion, "What must I do to enroll in your gym?" You happen to notice that the person is holding a Coca-Cola in one hand and a cigarette in the other, their eyes are bloodshot, and they reek of alcohol. Now, speaking for myself as a gym owner, before I entered into a dialogue about what the person would do once they joined the gym, I would first address what they needed to do before they joined the gym! I would say, "Listen friend, you need to stop smoking—stop drinking excessive amounts of alcohol—and stop drinking cans of sugar water."

It's the same thing when I counsel young people who show an interest in military and law enforcement careers. There are certain lifestyle choices that may need to be cut out of that person's life that could otherwise jeopardize the application process for unique positions of service within our community.

Returning to our Gospel, we notice what the rich man said in response to Jesus. The rich man told Jesus that he had kept the commands—in other words, he had already removed those acts from his life that at the most fundamental level would prohibit discipleship and real intimacy with God.

What was the response of Jesus to such a bold claim? Jesus looked at him with love (Mark 10:21). This is such a great detail that we cannot afford to miss it. The Scriptures teach us that God is love—not simply that God loves—but that *GOD IS LOVE* (1 John 4:8). And with the Love of God Himself, Jesus looks at the young man. This means that because God is love, a life with God is a life of total love—self-forgetting love—a love that starts with God, then radiates out into the lives of everyone whom our individual life comes into contact with.

Theologically, this is what it means to "sell everything you have." It's a call into radical love. It's an "all in" attitude. In our CrossFit analogy, it's no longer that we have a potential client coming to the threshold of the gym with a cigarette in hand—it's that same person who after a year of dedicated training now tells the coach—"OK, I've been at this for 365 days! Everything that was once a toxic and pollutant in my life has been removed—I'm ready for the big leagues! I want to go to the CrossFit Games!" Notice how the conversation changes at this point, doesn't it? It's no longer a matter of what NOT to do for this athlete—now it becomes altogether about WHAT YOU DO IN FACT DO!

And what, according to Jesus, do you do?

"If you want to be perfect, sell your possessions and give to the poor, and you will have treasure in heaven. Then come, follow me" (Matthew 19:21).

You throw it all away! And what do you throw away? Those possessions that make us who we think we are—and at the spiritual level—the greatest possessions we have are right between our ears—our thoughts. This is why the great theologian A. W. Tozer said, "The thoughts that come into your mind when you think about God are the most important thing about you." The Gospel compels us to change the way that we think about God, about ourselves, and about each other.

So let's focus the rest of our study together on what Jesus calls us to do in the *positive application* of the commandments.

We are privy to our Lord's teaching on the greatest commandment—this comes in Matthew, Chapter 22. When Jesus was asked what the greatest commandment was, He replied in a straightforward manner—to the point and with the authority of God Himself—by reciting the Shema.

The Shema is a prayer derived from a passage in the sixth chapter of the book of Deuteronomy. I'll write in here in Hebrew, which is probably the way Jesus would have said it: "*Sh'ma Yisrael Adonai Eloheinu Adonai Ehad.*" It means, "Hear, oh, Israel, the LORD our God, the LORD is one." It follows from this fundamental belief a moral imperative and anticipated response on our part—and the only appropriate response is found in the words of Jesus Christ Himself:

"Therefore, you shall love the Lord your God with all your heart, with all your soul, and with all your strength" (Matthew 22:37).

So what does the prayer mean? Notice the first word, *Shema*. "Hear." We are above all a people called upon to hear the *voice of God's Word*—and to have a personal, loving, and saving relationship with Jesus Christ—the Word and the Voice of God become flesh (John 1:14). This means that we don't set our own agenda. We don't determine our own path. We don't write our own story. We are akin to the rich man who asks Jesus, "What do I do?"

This biblical truth works against the grain of everything our American way of life teaches us from a very young age: freedom, self-determination, YES you can! Pick yourself up by your own bootstraps; even beyond our American way of life, the tendency of mankind to believe that we have to "work" for our "earnings" is an economic framework within our mind that spills over into our spiritual life. At the most fundamental level, this is the theological equivalent of mankind's attempt to create our own gods—the god of my own effort. The Bible teaches that anything can become a god—I mean, if the people of Israel once worshipped a golden calf, then clearly we can worship anything—including the god of our own ego. Mankind seems bent on the mantra of "I will write *my own story on my own* terms"—but as Christians, we must realize this is antagonistic to the Shema and the Commandment of Jesus.

The prayer of the Shema places us in the passive voice. We are spoken to by a power outside of ourselves. We stand in the shadow of the rich man before Jesus, eagerly awaiting our Lord's response.

In the negative sense, this means that God is not some vague force, some generic spiritual energy, some presence in the deep background of our life. Most importantly, this means that God is not something you can tap into whenever you happen to feel like it. In the positive sense, this means that God is as present to us as the air that we breathe. The Bible teaches that the presence of God Himself dwells within us, and, by His grace, we gradually become brighter and more beautiful as we become more like His Son, Jesus Christ (2 Corinthians 3:18).

OUR RESPONSE TO THE SHEMA

NOW, WHAT ARE THE BEHAVIORAL implications of the Shema—in other words, what is your response to the prayer as the one who hears the Word of God?

At the most fundamental level, the prayer teaches that we must love our LORD with the entirety of our being. God must be in some very real sense, the *only One* that we love: the one that we love above all things, with our whole heart, our whole soul, and all our strength.

Let's take these specifications one by one, just as Jesus taught.

The Shema says we must love God with our whole heart. In the Bible, the heart means the seat of our desires. In other words, we must love God with the totality of our emotions and our desires. God must be our one thing—the center of our gravity—the one thing in our life around which everything else in our life revolves.

How is this even possible? It's possible since God is the source, and the ground, and the goal of all things. As you've read in previous studies, Jesus Christ is not one prophet in a long lineage of prophets; He is not a spiritual guru; He is not another great moral teacher. This is entirely the wrong way to think about Christ.

Rather, the Bible teaches that Jesus is the fullness of the deity in bodily flesh (Colossians 2:9) and the exact representation of God's being (Hebrews 1:3). The Bible says that all things were made through Christ. For example, the Apostle John wrote that "Through Christ all things were made; without him nothing was made that has been made" (John 1:3). This means that God is the creative source of all that is: the Scriptures teach us that God is under all, in all, and through all (Ephesians 4:6). In the words of the Apostle Paul, "In God we live, and breathe, and have our being" (Acts 17:18).

For our purposes, this holds that if we desire things other than God Himself, we can still desire those things in a God-loving way—because we can desire God in, through, and under them.

A FEW RELATABLE EXAMPLES

YOU DESIRE TO GO TO THE CrossFit Box to work out. Good! There is nothing wrong with that. That's a good desire. But, in light of the Shema, you now see the beauty and complexity of CrossFit as strengthening your mind and focusing your will. You now see the combined power and grace of the functional movements demanded by the sport of CrossFit as reflective of the Power and Grace of God's being. In other words, your workout becomes worship.

Another example:

Are you a public safety officer or military operator who desires a profession of protection and service? That's also a good desire! However, in light of the Shema, you now see that there is no authority except what God has established (Romans 13:1). You realize that God has entrusted you to be a servant for good, and that as your profession may require others to submit to your authority, *you yourself* are submitted in mind, body, and spirit to *God Himself*.

Here's another example we can all relate to:

Do you desire a delicious dinner in the company of your loved ones? Good! Nothing wrong with that desire, either. But in light of the Shema, you now appreciate the food as something that strengthens you for God's service. In this sense, you can love God and chiefly desire God, even as you desire worldly things.

NOW LET'S MAKE THIS REAL

DO YOU LONG FOR JUSTICE IN our nation? Do you desire political righteousness and the accountability of those in power? Good! But we must see these pursuits and act on them as Jesus Christ Himself commanded. We must see justice and accountability as demands of God that ultimately lead back to the worship and praise of God Himself.

In addition to loving God with our heart, Jesus also commands that we love God with all our strength and our will. In the Bible, the strength and will of mankind always depict and call for the sacrifice of all that we have. In this sense, it is never our strength or our willpower that gets the job done—it is the strength of God, working in and through us. We are His instruments.

THE TOTALITY OF THE SHEMA

LET'S REVISIT THE GREATEST COMMANDMENT of Jesus Christ: Jesus replied, "Love the Lord your God with all your heart and with all your soul and with all your mind. This is the first and greatest commandment. And the second is like it: Love your neighbor as yourself" (Matthew 22:37–40).

The trajectory of the Shema leads us into the terrain of what our country most needs. Loving God compels—even demands—that we love each other. Everything in our life hinges on these two commands. Apart from obedience to these commands, nothing in our life—nothing within our circle of influence—can be right. Let's turn the coin over for the positive application: when you love God and others, then all the pieces (or as Jesus explained, all the extremities) of your life will fall perfectly into place.

The Bible teaches that through faith in Jesus Christ, we all become children of God. The tendency of our minds and the eyes in our head is to see patterns of complex differences. We systematically categorize things that we see as separate from other things that we see. However, we can learn to create new categories in our life. The question is *how we achieve this.*

The indwelling presence of Christ gives us a new mind, a new heart, even new eyes—Jesus gives us new ways of creating categories in our life. However, rather than categories that have historically *separated us*, Jesus provides a radical new category that *unites us*. In Jesus Christ, we are all One (Galatians 3:28). We are brothers and sisters. As one body of faithful believers we are told to Shema—to hear the voice of God—and to respond to it by loving God, and loving each other.

We return now to the beginning of our study—the rich man—who is every one of us in the Bible study today—asking Jesus Christ, "What must I do?"

Feel in your heart the Love of God looking upon you, and loving you just the way you are. What the Gospel teaches us is that rather than *doing something with an expectation of receiving something in return*, it's about *receiving something we do not deserve and cannot earn.*

Read this to yourself one more time, because this is the heart of the Gospel message: The Gospel teaches us that rather than *doing something with an expectation of receiving something in return*, it's about *receiving something we do not deserve and cannot earn.*

This is Grace, my brother and sisters, and it all begins with "confessing with your mouth that Jesus is Lord, and believing in your heart that God raised Him from the dead" (Romans 10:9).

YES and AMEN.

LESSON NINE

ON THE BATTLEFIELD OF LIFE

An Exposition of Paul's Prayer

for the Ephesians

LESSON NINE
ON THE BATTLEFIELD OF LIFE
An Exposition of Paul's Prayer for the Ephesians

Our Gospel reading today is from the Apostle Paul's letter to God's holy people in Ephesus (Paul's letter to the Ephesians).

THE WORD OF GOD:

I keep asking that the God of our Lord Jesus Christ, the glorious Father, may give you the Spirit of wisdom and revelation, so that you may know Him better. I pray that the eyes of your heart may be enlightened in order that you may know the hope to which He has called you, the riches of His glorious inheritance in His holy people, and His incomparably great power for us who believe.

(Ephesians 1:17–19)

MY BROTHERS AND MY SISTERS, may the grace of our Lord Jesus Christ, the love of God, and the fellowship of the Holy Spirit, be with you (2 Corinthians 13:14). I want to study with you today the topic of *The Battlefield of Life*. Early in my military career, a longtime mentor of mine pulled me aside and said, "Greg, good leaders are able to reveal things to subordinates that they could otherwise never see on their own." His words resonated deep within my soul, and I was held captive by the idea that something obvious to me could be seemingly invisible to someone else. The implications on the battlefield were immense: unless I opened the eyes of my soldiers and helped them see potential dangers within their midst, catastrophic injury would surely be their end. However, once the danger was revealed to them, their "battlefield knowledge" increased, and they would be more likely to navigate risk independent of my supervision. And perhaps even more encouraging, with their newfound wisdom, the subordinate soldier would be in a position to help reveal to their peers what they would never see on their own.

In many respects and to varying degrees, we are all soldiers on the battlefield of life. Twists, turns, peaks, and valleys are part of the terrain we need to successfully navigate in order to reach our final destination.

However, in addition to dangerous valleys, there are also magnificent mountaintops that our soul longs to summit. Yet, unless revealed to us by a trusted source of wisdom and knowledge much greater than ourselves, the tendency is to rely on our independent understanding, which often leads to a closed loop of crisscrossing back and forth across the dark valleys of life.

I recall learning the fundamentals of land navigation during U.S. Army Basic Officer Leadership Training in the hills of North Dakota. During daylight hours, the task was fairly simple. Given a compass and map, I navigated across open terrain to specific points or "plots" that my instructor had assigned me. However, in the pitch-black night, unable to see the tips of my fingers with my arm outstretched, the task became altogether impossible. On one particular night, and very characteristic of North Dakota summers, there was a great lightning storm. Although startling and a bit nerve-racking, I soon discovered the lightning was a blessing in disguise. When it struck, it was much like a flare bursting in the night. The terrain all around me was instantly illuminated. For a few seconds, the imprint of my surroundings made an impression on my mind. I could essentially "see in the dark." Although brief, those momentary intervals of revelation of my surroundings were enough to allow me to successfully complete the navigation course.

THE POWER OF VISION

IN THE BOOK OF PROVERBS, it says, "Where there is no vision, the people perish" (Proverbs 29:18). In order to navigate the battlefield of life, we need to clearly identify the obstacles before us. However, as my mentor counseled me years ago, we also need a trusted source to reveal to us what we could otherwise not see on our own. The idea of "not being able to see on our own" is elaborated on in the Bible with these words: "Be not wise in thy own eyes" (Proverbs 3:7). In other words, if we rely on our own understanding, knowledge, and worldly acquired wisdom, we will not be able to see clearly.

The potential pitfall and shortcoming of limited understanding and "battlefield blindness" was certainly at the heart of the Apostle Paul in his letter to the Ephesians. In Ephesians 1:17, we read, "I pray that the God of our Lord Jesus Christ, the Father of glory, might give you spiritual wisdom and revelation in the knowledge of Him." In other words, Paul's prayer was that God would grant us a specific type of spiritual wisdom we could otherwise never arrive at on our own.

We may interpret through verse 17 that Paul was specifically describing a type of wisdom that could only be achieved through the power and working of the Holy Spirit. Paul specifically prayed that the Ephesians would experience a supernatural endowment of wisdom that would be achieved through God's revelation of Himself. Paul's contention, therefore, was to ensure the believer understood that worldly wisdom, gained through the intellect of humanity, would never be enough to truly know the "surpassing greatness" of God. Paul's use of the term "revelation" referred to God's own self-disclosure, which would be experienced supernaturally by the believer.

In the New Testament Epistle of James, the author made clear the distinction between wisdom of the world and wisdom revealed by God. James describes worldly wisdom as "earthly, unspiritual and demonic" (James 3:15–16). In the context of navigating the battlefield of life, the result of following and "seeing" through the eyes of our own wisdom is like a landmine waiting to be stepped upon. A torrential explosion of "envy, selfish ambition, disorder and evil" (James 3:15–16) is dangerously underfoot. The Apostle Paul foresaw the treacherous terrain that the Ephesians, in addition to future believers, would need to safely transverse, and through his prayer, Paul's hope was that God would reveal Himself to us. Through this supernatural revelation, our wisdom and knowledge would be increased to heavenly proportion, which is distinctly different and abundantly more important than worldly wisdom.

James articulated this difference in verse 3:17: "Wisdom that comes from heaven is first of all pure; then peace-loving, considerate, submissive, full of mercy and good fruit, impartial and sincere." With this newfound perspective of "Heavenly wisdom" held in mind, we turn once again to the beauty and magnitude of the opening line of Paul's prayer. With gratitude in our heart, we discover that Paul prayed that you and I would have a direct experience of the power and glory of God. Like a flash of lightning in the middle of a dark night, Paul's prayer was such that we would experience an imprint of God on our minds and hearts, and that through this divine revelation, our spiritual wisdom would be increased.

THE EYES OF THE HEART

THE SECOND COMPONENT OF PAUL'S prayer for the Ephesians was equally inspiring and complemented the revelation of God invoked in verse 17. Paul prayed, "Since the eyes of your heart have been enlightened, that you would know what is the hope of His calling, what are the riches of the glory of His inheritance in the saints." By focusing on Paul's use of the word "heart" in this verse, and through an understanding of the bodily function of the heart, we can truly appreciate the magnitude of Paul's prayer.

Because you were made in the image of God, you have an ordained birthright and divine capacity to know and *experience* the presence of God. Before going any further, let us turn our attention to the words of Jesus, who said, "This is eternal life, *that they may know you*, the one true God, and Jesus Christ, whom you have sent" (John 17:3). Oftentimes when reading the Bible and the words of Jesus, it is equally important to note what Jesus said in addition to what *Jesus did not say*. Therefore, take special consideration that Jesus's prayer was for you and me to *know God*. He did not say, "Know *about* God." In other words, Jesus's prayer and hope was that you and I would have a direct experience and firsthand knowledge of God. And now, through the words of Paul in Ephesians verse 1:17, we arrive at the understanding that this knowledge of God will not be possible through our own understanding or human intellect. Knowing God is a supernatural experience, which is the direct result of God revealing Himself to us.

In the context of any personal relationship, this makes total and complete sense. No matter how hard we might try, in order to really know someone, they ultimately need to reveal their mind and soul to us. This specific type of "revelation," understood through verse 18 of Paul's prayer, was experienced within the "eyes of our heart" that were enlightened through the revelation of God. In the same manner in which our mind has thinking, reasoning, and intellectual capacities, Paul understood that our heart shared these capacities on an even deeper and more spiritually significant level. In fact, according to Paul, the mind may have even blunted the true spiritual wisdom of the heart.

In his letter to the Corinthians, Paul wrote, "Their minds are made dull because a veil covers their hearts" (2 Corinthians 3:14–15). We can interpret through Ephesians 1:17–18 that Paul's prayer for the believer was to "see" that if truth, wisdom, and knowledge about God were to be faithfully grasped, then the heart must be enlightened. Furthermore, as the heart is a central and life-sustaining organ of the body, it is responsible for circulating both blood and oxygen throughout the entire cellular system. Thus, when Paul prays for the "eyes of our heart to be enlightened," he is praying that in addition to knowing *about* God at the intellectual level of our mind, that through the circulation of God's love throughout every cell of our body, we would be "enlightened" to truly *know God* by the revelation of His presence. Finally, it is important to note that in the Bible, the word "heart" often referred to the genuine self, as distinguished from appearance, identification with the mind, and physical presence.[7] And this "heart self" had its own nature, character, and disposition, which ultimately affected the thoughts, words, and actions of the believer.[8] Therefore, a believer whose "heart" was illuminated by the revelation of God would radically change the entire makeup of their life and would never be the same again.

Because of the tendency of our human intellect to attach through the senses to material objects and "desires of the flesh" (Galatians 5:17), Paul's prayer centered on *spiritual* acquisition. For example, we observed that in verse 17, Paul's hope was that we would acquire *spiritual wisdom* in the knowledge of God. Through the revelation of God in our lives, the eyes of our heart would be enlightened, allowing us to faithfully see what truly mattered most. Therefore, as we continue to journey though the totality of Paul's prayer, we observe the "riches" that Paul desires that we both see and inherit are meant to be enjoyed spiritually and not worldly.

We take note that verse 18 concludes with Paul's use of the word *inheritance*. This word is of immense importance and is best understood through the context of the Old Testament. Time and time again, we note that God referred to His creation as His own inheritance. In Deuteronomy, we read that God took His

[7] Walter Elwell and Barry J. Beitzel, "Wisdom, Wisdom Literature," in *Baker Encyclopedia of the Bible* (Grand Rapids, MI: Baker Book House, 1988), p. 2149.
[8] *Baker Encyclopedia of the Bible*, p. 2149.

creation, "As the people of His inheritance" (Deuteronomy 4:20) and that God's people were "His own inheritance, redeemed by His great power" (Deuteronomy 9:26). As sons and daughters of God, our relationship with Him is similar to that of Father and child. The intimacy of this relationship is absolutely vital for us to comprehend, and was at the heart of Jesus's ministry. In the first two words of the "Lord's Prayer," Jesus explained the nature of our relationship with God by the declaration, "Our Father" (Matthew 6:9). In this manner, Jesus invoked our understanding of the divine connection to our "Father of glory." Jesus embraced and perfectly articulated the magnitude of this relationship and his divine right to the inheritance of his Father when he declared, "All I have is yours, and all you have is mine" (John 17:10).

Paul's prayer as expressed in verse 18 is therefore twofold. First, his hope is that we would embrace our relationship with God as that of Father and child. Second, through the context of this Fatherly relationship and through spiritual revelation, Paul prayed that we would embrace our true inheritance as sons and daughters of God. It is exceedingly important to take note of Paul's use of the word *glory*, which is evident in verses 17 and 18. In verse 17, God was declared to be the "Father of glory." Throughout the Old Testament, the glory of God was oftentimes so bright and of such overwhelming power that it was shrouded in a cloud (Exodus 16:10). In verse 18, we discover that the brilliance and intensity of God's glory is to be shared with us as a component of our inheritance as children of God.

THE SURPASSING GREATNESS OF GOD

IN VERSE NINETEEN OF PAUL'S prayer, we take special note of the connection between the "surpassing greatness" and power of God, in direct proportion toward those who believe in Him, and "what is the surpassing greatness of His power towards us who believe, in accordance with the working of the strength of His might." As described by Paul, it was according to one's level of belief, which was furthermore achieved only through God's revelation of Himself, that a believer could fully experience the "strength of His might." Paul's use of the phrase "surpassing greatness," when understood within the context of navigating the battlefield of life, is worthy of our thankfulness and delight. *Surpassing* can best be understood as "superior," or ranking higher than any other type of power, regardless of how immense our intellect may attempt to convince us it is. The magnificent, supreme, and nearly incomprehensible power of God's greatness is directed with love toward those who believe in Him. Through God's own revelation of Himself, we may thus be faithfully "inherited" into His enduring love and embrace.

CONCLUDING THOUGHTS

NAVIGATING THE BATTLEFIELD OF LIFE can be a treacherous task, full of unsuspecting danger. However, this same battlefield, when faithfully illuminated, can become a place of beauty and spiritual splendor. In order for the terrain around us to become visible, a transformation will need to take place within both our mind and our heart. The biblical word "grace" was described to me once as the "effect of God giving us what we do not deserve," and "mercy" taking place when "God *does not give us* what we do deserve." Paul's prayer invokes this very measure of grace in his hope that you and I would experience the revelation of God, and through this supernatural opening and enlightenment of the "eyes of our heart," we would fully embrace our right to an inheritance of epic proportion.

YES and AMEN.

LESSON TEN

WITNESSING THE GIFT OF THE HOLY SPIRIT

LESSON TEN
WITNESSING THE GIFT OF THE HOLY SPIRIT

THE WORD OF GOD

And when the day of Pentecost came, they were all together in one place. Suddenly a sound like the blowing of a violent wind came from heaven and filled the whole house where they were sitting. They saw what seemed to be tongues of fire that separated and came to rest on each of them. And they were all filled with the Holy Spirit and began to speak in other tongues (or languages) as the Spirit enabled them.

(Acts 2:1–4)

MY BROTHERS AND MY SISTERS, may the grace of our Lord Jesus Christ, the love of God, and the fellowship of the Holy Spirit, be with you (2 Corinthians 13:14). I want to study with you today the magnificent topic of *Witnessing the Gift of the Holy Spirit*. Jesus Christ's last words to His disciples were, "But you will receive power when the Holy Spirit has come upon you, and *you will be my witness* in Jerusalem and in all Judea and Samaria, and to the ends of the earth" (Acts 1:8–9—my emphasis). Although in this context our Lord was specifically addressing the apostles, the Bible teaches that the promise of the Holy Spirit is freely available for every believer in Jesus Christ (Acts 2:38–39). All believers in Jesus receive the gift of the Holy Spirit at the moment of their conversion (Acts 2:38; Romans 5:5; Galatians 3:2). This means that when a believer confesses their sin and asks for God's forgiveness, they become a new person—not by their own deeds, works, or merit, but by the gracious work of God's Holy Spirit (Ephesians 2:9).[9] To use the terminology of our Lord, the believer is "born again" (John 3:3–7).

---

[9] Dr. Harold Sala. *Getting Acquainted with the Holy Spirit* (Mandaluyong City, Manila: OMF Literature, Inc., 2017), p. 58.

The Apostle Paul further elaborated on the supernatural "born again" new life of the Christian: "If anyone is in Christ, he is a new creation. The old has passed away; behold, the new has come (2 Corinthians 5:17). The moment the believer looks to Christ as Lord and Savior, the Holy Spirit comes to indwell their body, making it a "temple of the Holy Spirit" (1 Corinthians 6:19–20; cf., 2 Corinthians 6:16). According to Jesus, this transformational experience results in a *receipt of power* that enables the believer *to be a witness* of the Gospel message to the ends of the earth. This all boils down to one amazing promise, one astonishing mission, and one breathtaking responsibility for the individual believer and collective Body of Christ.

ARE OUR LORD'S EXPECTATIONS BEING MET?

I FIND THAT I MUST DRAW on a theological query from the great mind of author and pastor Francis Chan. Based on the inerrant *Word of God*, we have confidence that the *Spirit of God* dwells within every believer, which effectually makes every Christian a living and breathing *Temple of God's Holy Spirit* (1 Corinthians 3:16, 6:19). This being the case, then shouldn't there be a measurable and observable difference between the regenerated person who has the very Spirit of God within them, and another person who does not?[10] Although by conversion Christians can declare that they are *born again* and *dead to sin but alive in Christ* (Romans 6:3–8), we must caution ourselves against the possibility that these words have become nothing more than the parroted teaching of biblical doctrine. In other words, if someone outside the Body of Christ began to notice that there was no fundamental change or difference in the life of a converted person, then are believers truly *witnessing our faith* as our Lord commanded?

---

[10] This "theological question" was brought to my attention in Francis Chan's book The Forgotten God–*Reversing Our Tragic Neglect of the Holy Spirit* (Colorado Springs, CO: David C. Cook. 2009), p. 32.

The late author and minister Martyn Lloyd-Jones once pointed out that there is a vast difference between being a *witness for Jesus and an advocate for Jesus*.[11] Whereas a great many people today are quite content to be an advocate of the Christian faith, only a few actively witness their spiritual gifts for the purpose of edifying the Body of Christ. Furthermore, many churches seem to be more concerned with filling pews and developing new programs than in proclaiming the transformational power of a Spirit-filled life.[12] Reasoning from this fact, perhaps now is the time for renewed urgency in addressing the concern of A. W. Tozer: "The whole level of spirituality among us is low—the incentive to seek the higher plateaus in the things of the Spirit is all but gone."[13]

In his acclaimed book, The Forgotten God, Francis Chan argued that "there is a desperate need in the church for the Holy Spirit of God to be given room to have His way."[14] Similar to the uneasiness felt by Tozer's observation of the generally low level of spirituality among Christians, Chan's sentiment that the Church is in desperate need of the Holy Spirit ought to compel the Body of Christ to question what's gone wrong. After all, according to the Apostle Paul, the Spirit of God dwells in believers (Romans 8:9), effectually making every individual follower of Christ a physical tabernacle of God's Spirit (1 Corinthians 3:16, 6:19–20). This means that the individual believer's body is the Spirit of God's temple—we are His dwelling place (John 14:23). Continuing this line of reasoning, Paul explained that "just as a body, though one, has many parts, but all its parts form one body, so it is with Christ" (1 Corinthians 12:12). In other words, if each individual believer is a temple, then the spiritual power of the collective Body of Christ should turn the world upside down. On the basis thereof, how are we to reconcile the declaration of the biblical testimony with the troubling observations of such influential ministers of God's Word as Chan and Tozer?

---

[11] Sala, p. 34. The Blue Letter Bible defines *witness* in the context of Acts 1:8 in the ethical sense as, "Those who after his example have proved the strength and genuineness of their faith in Christ by undergoing a violent death."
[12] Sala, p. 31.
[13] A. W. Tozer. Quoted in Francis Chan's book, *The Forgotten God–Reversing Our Tragic Neglect of the Holy Spirit* (Colorado Springs, CO: David C. Cook. 2009), p. 27.
[14] Chan, p. 27. Chan's book *Forgotten God* reached the New York Times bestseller top 10 list for 10 consecutive weeks.

MAKING ROOM FOR THE SPIRIT

IN THE SPORT OF OLYMPIC WEIGHTLIFTING, few masters of the barbell have achieved the worldwide respect and admiration as that of Coach Mike Burgener.[15] In the CrossFit community, legend has it that when Coach Burgener walks into the gym, everyone in attendance on that particular day gain's five pounds on their former personal weightlifting records (a huge increase in strength considering that many weightlifting world records are set in increments of one-half pounds). Coach Burgener says nothing, offers no technical cues, nor demonstrates any particular hidden insights on the fundamental principles of the snatch or clean and jerk. How then do people account for the near instantaneous increase in strength?

Based on the testimony of hundreds of gym owners (each gym owner represents approximately 100 athletes), it can only be attributed to a combination of Mike's presence in the gym and his immediate proximity to each individual athlete.[16] Although seemingly impossible to quantify, ordinary people and world-class weightlifters alike increase in strength simply because they spend time in the presence of Coach Burgener. In all humility, Coach Burgener explains the phenomenon by saying that "people increase in strength because they *think then can*." This account certainly begs the question—if people gain physical strength in the presence of a person who compels them to *think they can*, then how much more should believers manifest the miraculous gifts of the Spirit when God Himself dwells within them?

For our purposes of understanding the work of the Holy Spirit, this particular illustration has immense relevance. In fact, the spiritual principle involved is exactly what we read about in the book of Acts. In describing what happened when John and Peter went on trial before the Sanhedrin, Luke wrote, "When they saw the courage of Peter and John and realized that they were unschooled,

---

[15] Mike Burgener's oldest son Casey broke the national record for the snatch at the 2004 Olympic Trials and won gold in the 2008 Pan American Championships.

[16] In addition to the sport of weightlifting, I have experienced similar testimonies from professional boxers who have trained under master-level trainers and coaches. Most recently, six-time world champion Robert "The Ghost" Guerrero commented that the ringside presence of his dad (Ruben Guerrero and Robert's longtime coach) has propelled him to victories that were otherwise seemingly impossible.

ordinary men, they were astonished and they took note that these men had *been with Jesus* (Acts 4:13—my emphasis). It was not about books, laws, regulations, or moral lessons (or in the weightlifting analogy, coaching cues, tips, or physical demonstrations). What set Peter and John apart was the fact that they had been with Jesus—*and they had stayed with Him* (John 1:37–39). And in the process, Jesus had completely transformed their lives.

In the Apostle John's beautiful account of our Lord's conversation with His first two disciples (John 1:35–42), we are witness to the Gospel-centered transformation that awaits those people who *stay with Jesus*. When our Lord asked the two men, "What do you want?" (John 1:38a), they immediately responded by asking a question of their own: "Rabbi, where are you staying?" (John 1:38b). How interesting to answer a question with a question—not to mention the seemingly mindless quality of the question. To ask where Jesus is staying? Couldn't these two former disciples of John the Baptist have come up with a more profound question? After all, here is the Lord of the universe asking, "What do you want? What are you looking for?" And they answer by asking, "Where are you staying?"

But I propose their instincts were in fact completely right. When Jesus was on the earth, His presence was limited to His physical and spatial locality. In this sense, in order for the first disciples to *stay with Jesus*, they needed to be physically in His presence. However, for the followers of Christ after His ascension to the Father, we now experience personal fellowship with Him through the Holy Spirit every moment of our life (Romans 8:9–11; Galatians 2:19-20; Titus 3:4–6). This means that Jesus Christ, as much as the Father, is the indwelling presence of God within every regenerated Christian believer—but only through the Spirit of God.[17] To this effect, Paul explained, "Anyone who does not have the Spirit of Christ, that person does not belong to him" (Romans 8:9) and believers are "dead to sin but alive to God" (Romans 6:11—MSG).

---

[16] My interviews with gym owners took place between the years of 2012 and 2014 during my worldwide travels teaching the CrossFit Goal Setting and Positive Self-Talk course.

[17] M. Turner in T. Desmond Alexander's *The New Dictionary of Biblical Theology–Holy Spirit* (Downers Grove, IL: InterVarsity Press, 2000), p. 550.

Paul's logic would seem to suggest that when the Spirit of God dwells within the believer there should be a significant difference between that person and a non-Christian. But is this in fact the case in the life of the individual believer and the Body of Christ?

THE CENTER AND ITS CONTRAST[18]

THE BIBLE TEACHES THAT A life in the Spirit is what God desires for all Christians. At the moment of conversion, the Holy Spirit indwells believers, guiding them, sanctifying them, and empowering them for work in God's Kingdom (Romans 8:2–17). The notion that Christians are *in the Spirit*, and that the *Spirit dwells in them*, was such an important theological idea for the Apostle Paul that he reinforced it three times in his letter to the Romans (Romans 8:9–11), and succinctly culminated his argument with the resounding statement: "For those who are led by the Spirit of God are the children of God" (Romans 8:14).

The Apostle Paul's theology of the Holy Spirit has led Evangelical Christians around the world to share the doctrine that the Spirit is active in the lives of all believers.[19] A believer's first experience with the Spirit of God takes place within their heart the moment they put their faith in Christ. Emphasizing this very point, in his book, *The Small Catechism*, Martin Luther described the initial work of the Holy Spirit in his heart as essential to his conversion experience by saying, "I believe that I cannot by my own reason or strength believe in Jesus Christ, my Lord, or come to Him but the Holy Ghost has called me by the gospel."[20] Echoing Luther's sentiment on the Holy Spirit, the great theologian J. I. Packer wrote, "Without the Spirit there would not be a Christian in the world."[21]

---

[18] The idea for this particular part of the study title and the accompanying organizational framework were brought to my attention in Gregory Boyd's book, *Across the Spectrum* (Grand Rapids, MI: Baker Academic, 2009).

[19] Timothy Tennent. *Theology in the context of World Christianity* (Grand Rapids, MI: Zondervan, 2007), p. 166.

[20] Quoted in Mollie Ziegler Hemingway's piece "Faith Unbounded," *Christianity Today*, September 9, 2010, p. 74.

[21] J. I. Packer, *Knowing God* (London: Hodder & Stoughton, 1984), p. 79.

The Apostle Paul masterfully treats the issue of the believer's first experience with the Holy Spirit in 1 Corinthians 12:13: "For we were all baptized by one Spirit so as to form one body—whether Jews or Gentiles, slave or free—and we were all given one Spirit to drink." In this theologically packed verse, Paul makes four remarkable points: First, the baptism applies to all believers; second, all believers are baptized by the same Spirit; third, believers are baptized into the Body of Christ; and fourth, the baptism and union with the Body of Christ take place *at the moment of conversion*. This means that when a new believer "confesses with their mouth that Jesus Christ is Lord, and believes in their heart that God raised Jesus from the dead" (Romans 10:9), they receive the indwelling power of the Holy Spirit (John 14:17), a new heart (Titus 3:5), and are incorporated into the Body of Christ (1 Corinthians 12:13).[22] Paul seems to suggest throughout his theological treatment on baptism that Christians become members of Christ's body by being baptized into it by the Spirit—and that this supernatural experience is either equivalent to conversion or simultaneous with it. [23]

This being the case, how do we account for cases in Acts where there was clearly a separation between conversion (or regeneration) and a subsequent baptism of the Spirit? The Pentecostals substantiate much of their doctrine based on the account in Acts 2, which records that on the day of Pentecost the Holy Spirit descended onto the Body of Christ in the form of "tongues of fire" and empowered those that received it for special service and bold witness (Acts 2:2–4). To account for what might otherwise be accepted as the norm, esteemed theologian Millard Erickson argues that Acts covers a transitional period in the life of the church.[24] Although he acknowledges that in certain cases there was indeed a lapse of time between regeneration and the receipt of the Holy Spirit, these instances involved the last of the Old Testament believers who were regenerate because of the revelation they received and their faith in God. [25]

---

[22] Dr. Gerry Breshears, Western Seminary TH503 outline on the Holy Spirit.
[23] Millard Erickson, *Christian Theology* (Grand Rapids, MI: Baker Academic, 2013), p. 801.
[24] Erickson, p. 801.
[25] Erickson, p. 801.

The issue of an immediate or post-conversion experience with the Spirit (in contrast with a more gradual *filling of the Spirit*) is significant and affects nearly every area of the Christian life. Accessing the biblical arguments on both sides of the equation leads us to a fundamental theological and doctrinal question: Should believers anticipate (and in this sense actively seek out and pray for) a subsequent filling of the Spirit beyond their initial conversion experience? Furthermore, to what degree would this unique and distinct second encounter with the Spirit be objectively recognizable in the manifestation of miraculous spiritual gifts? And perhaps most important, to what extent should speaking in tongues be associated with the first evidence of a Second Baptism?

UNDERSTANDING PENTECOSTALISM

IN THE PENTECOSTAL TRADITION, many hold that a postconversion (or postregeneration) experience, often referred to as, "the baptism in (or with) the Holy Spirit," will take place in the life of the believer.[26] Evidence of this unmistakable moment commonly manifests itself in the believer's life through a full range of gifts and miraculous manifestations of the Spirit that were evident during the era of the New Testament.[27] Pentecostal and Charismatic Christian theology teach that believers should look forward to an experience of the Holy Spirit—and unique sign-gifts of the Spirit—subsequent to their initial conversion.

The *Foundations of Pentecostal Theology* emphasizes, "The Baptism of the Holy Ghost is a definite experience, subsequent to salvation, whereby the Third Person of the Godhead comes upon the believer to anoint and energize him for special service."[28] This same body of doctrine holds that although "baptism with the Holy Ghost was given once and for all, as far as the Church in general is concerned" it does not necessarily mean that every believer is immediately *filled with the Spirit* upon conversion.[29] The Baptism in the Holy

---

[26] Tennent, p. 166.
[27] Gregory Boyd, *Across the Spectrum* (Grand Rapids, MI: Baker Publishing, 2009), p. 237.
[28] Breshears, Western Seminary TH503 outline on the Holy Spirit.
[29] Breshears, Western Seminary TH503 outline on the Holy Spirit.

Spirit is meant to empower believers for greater acts of service within the Body of Christ. This being the case, the full range of Spirit-empowered gifts of healing, prophecy, tongues, and miraculous powers (1 Corinthians 12:7–11) are available for believers today and should be actively sought after (1 Corinthians 12:31a).

THE GIFTS SHALL CEASE

A MORE CONSERVATIVE BAPTIST THEOLOGY would point to the fact that very often proponents for a Second Baptism and "sign-gifts" tend to overly focus on 1 Corinthians 12:31a, which states, "Now eagerly desire the greater gifts" while completely dismissing the continuing thought of Paul to "seek the most excellent way" (1 Corinthians 12:31b). And what was Paul's "most excellent way?" It was love! Paul emphatically explained that no matter how great the apparent "sign-gift" was in the believer's life, it amounted to nothing if the believer did not have love (1 Corinthians 13:1–3). This means that the real evidence of the Spirit at work in the believer's life is the *fruit of the Spirit itself*—"faith, hope and love. But the greatest of these is love" (1 Corinthians 13:13). Baptists teach that every Christian receives the Spirit at conversion (1 Corinthians 12:13), and that speaking in tongues or any other objective "sign-gift evidence" are not intended to be the normal effectual work of the Spirit within the believer's life. Rather, Christ gives the Spirit the moment He welcomes individuals into God's family through faith and repentance (Acts 2:38).

In addition to addressing the possibility that Paul taught that the gifts would cease, many theologians make a similar argument based on Hebrews 2:3–4, namely that the purpose of the "signs, wonders and various miracles" (Hebrews 2:4a) of the Holy Spirit was to authenticate the revelation of Jesus Christ. Given that the final revelation is now freely available in the completed canon of Scripture, the gifts have ceased. This line of reasoning seems to be supported by the Apostle John who explained that the purpose of our Lord's "signs in the presence of his disciples" was so that Christians would "believe that Jesus is the Messiah" (John 20:30–31). In other words, Cessationist theology would contend that the purpose of the miraculous gifts was to testify to the life and divinity of Christ in addition to our Lord's first apostles (Acts 2:34).

This unique and historic purpose having once been fulfilled, the miraculous gifts become unnecessary and subsequently faded out of the Church.[30]

New Testament scholar William Barclay makes a compelling argument for Cessationist theology by suggesting that the miracles of the early church were needed as a guarantee of the truth and power of the Gospel message. Furthermore, the apostles had uniquely benefited from personal contact with Jesus, empowering them for miraculous gifts and service in a way never to be repeated following their death. This, combined with a general atmosphere of expectancy of the Lord's imminent return, contributed to the supernatural presence of spiritual gifts.[31] As an afterthought, Barclay then proposes the question, "But have miracles in fact stopped?" A visit to any first-world emergency room would reveal doctors and surgeons doing common things that in apostolic times would have been seen as so *uncommon* they would be immediately regarded as a miracle. In this sense, for Christians, miracles are all around us when we have eyes to see them.

WRESTLING WITH THE EVIDENCE

WE NOW TURN OUR ATTENTION to addressing the implications and considerations raised by both sides of the dispute. However, before doing so, I suggest that we set aside for a moment the particular issue of a distinct Second Baptism to wrestle with what appears to be the intimate cause and effect relationship between a subsequent encounter with the Holy Spirit and the evidence of the encounter made manifest through particular spiritual gifts. (As mentioned above, many hold that the initial evidence will be speaking in tongues). In other words, is one possible without the other? The potential danger in holding to a doctrine that teaches that objective and tangible evidence of a Second Baptism is to be expected is that a believer may be unintentionally compelled to focus

---

[30] Erickson, p. 800.
[31] William Barclay, *The Acts of the Apostles New Daily Study Bible* (Louisville, KY: Westminster John Knox Press, 2003), p. 36.

on the gifts (the evidence) of the experience, rather than the actual encounter with the Holy Spirit Himself.

By way of an illustration, imagine a parent who loves their child so much they are compelled—out of love—to give their child a gift. The child, upon receiving the gift, is then compelled to love the *giver of the gift* more than the gift itself. I believe this is an apt example of the exchange that takes place in the life of the Christian. Our Heavenly Father is eager to pour out into the lives of His children a great many gifts (James 1:17). This means that on one hand, as children of God, we should eagerly anticipate and pray for His gifts. However, on the other hand (and arguably more important) we should seek greater intimacy with God—the giver of the gift rather than focusing solely on the gift itself. As Erickson so eloquently pointed out, "It is not a matter of getting more of the Holy Spirit—it is, rather, a matter of His possessing more of our lives."[32]

Returning then to the matter of spiritual gifts, we can glean a great deal of wisdom from a close study of the Apostle Paul's exposition on the matter. First and foremost, the gifts are bestowed on the Body of Christ and are therefore meant for the edification of the *entire Body* rather than the enrichment (or boasting!) of an individual member of the Body (1 Corinthians 12:7). Second, the gifts are intended for use in cooperation with other believers, meaning that not one person has all the gifts (1 Corinthians 12:28–30). This is why Paul explained that each member of the Church is crucial for the Body of the Church to function properly. This logic leads Paul to elaborate on the fact that all the gifts of the Spirit are important (1 Corinthians 12:22–26), and that the Holy Spirit "distributes them just as He determines" (1 Corinthians 12:11).

In 1 Corinthians 12:13, Paul emphasizes the point that "One Spirit forms one body."[33] Whether of the more conservative or the liberal theological camp, Paul's emphasis on the "*one Spirit*" holds remarkable implications in the believer's life. Paul makes the case that the same "one Spirit" that raised Jesus from the

---

[32] Erickson, p. 802.
[33] My use of italics in this verse to emphasize the unity of God in the Spirit and to accentuate my argument made throughout the remainder of the paragraph.

dead comes to dwell within the believer at the moment of their conversion (Romans 6:10–11). This particular verse should therefore be of resounding encouragement and comfort for all believers, because without this assurance, a new Christian could be led to think there needs to be a dramatic experience with the Holy Spirit in order for their conversion to "be real." Needless to say, this uncertainty is unhealthy in the life of the Christian and may lead to self-doubt, and even worse, fabricated testimonials about Spirit activity and encounters.

All this being said, it is equally important to heed the fact that Paul expected all Christians to "be filled with the Spirit" (Ephesians 5:18). Paul contrasts being "Spirit filled" with being "wine-filled." The former leads to glorifying God and the Body of Christ, the later to debauchery and foolishness. Being "filled with the Spirit" implies the action is ongoing and continual. However, rather than being led to think this means that we effectually need "more of the Spirit," I think it means that we are to surrender more of our lives to Him. As Christians, we are called to give the Holy Spirit full control over every area of our life. After all, this in and of itself is the primary gift of the Holy Spirit—the Holy Spirit Himself.[34]

CESSATIONISM AND CONTINUATIONISM—
THE HISTORY OF THE CHURCH

OVER THE YEARS THERE HAVE been differing views on the active role of the Holy Spirit continuing to perform miracles such as divine healing, prophecy, and most notably, speaking in tongues. Generally speaking, four different views have been proposed to include *Cessationism, Functional Cessationism, Continuationism,* and *Word-Faith.* For our purposes, a brief overview of the first three positions (the *Word-Faith* movement is outside the scope of our discussion) is helpful in creating a framework for understanding the church's historical positions on Second Baptism and spiritual gifts.

---

[34] Breshears, Spiritual Gifts Position Paper. Grace Community Church, Gresham, OR.

Continuationism holds that while Scripture is God's only trustworthy voice, He continues to speak to Churches and individuals through His Spirit. These unique revelations of His Word must be tested and weighed against the Bible. In addition, God continues to perform miracles (which may include speaking in tongues) and believers should pray for and expect these miracles to be a present reality within their life and the Body of Christ.[35] Continuationism holds that believers in Jesus Christ should expect (and look forward to) an experience of the Holy Spirit after their initial conversion. This distinct second blessing results in the manifestation of spiritual gifts in the believer's life.

In the Pentecostal tradition, this experience is commonly referred to as the "Baptism in the Spirit." According to this view, the primary objective evidence of the Holy Spirit baptism is speaking in tongues and empowerment for service in God's Kingdom.[36] Those who hold this view substantiate their position by noting that in Acts 2, the disciples "were filled with the Holy Spirit and began to speak in other tongues as the Spirit enabled them" (Acts 2:4). Because the disciples had been followers of Jesus for nearly three years, in addition to the fact that in John 20:22, "Jesus breathed on them (the disciples) and said, 'Receive the Holy Spirit," the logical conclusion is that there is a distinct Second Baptism. In other words, John 20:22 clearly establishes one baptism, whereas Acts 2:4 establishes another. The difference in Acts 2:4 (the Second Baptism) is that there is *objective evidence* of the Holy Spirit's work within the believer which is made manifest in *glossalilia*—speaking in unknown human languages.

Perhaps the strongest biblical evidence for Continuationism is the careful exegetical reading of 1 Corinthians 13:8–12. The Cessationist has historically connected the verse, "But when completeness comes, what is in part disappears" (1 Corinthians 13:10), to the close of the biblical canon, and concludes that miraculous gifts are no longer necessary or operational. In other words, the "completeness" in this particular verse is the complete canon of Scripture, which Paul foretold would result in the cessation of prophecy, tongues, and words of

[35] Breshears, Western Seminary TH503 outline on Holy Spirit.
[36] Tennent, p. 167.

knowledge (1 Corinthians 13:8). However, a more through understanding of Paul's theology on spiritual gifts demonstrates that completeness is in fact the eternal state ushered in at the second coming of Christ. Furthermore, when Paul speaks in verse 12 of seeing "face to face," he most likely is referring to the eternal state, subsequent to the return of Christ.[37] Finally, it is vital to pay close attention to Paul's explicitly stated purpose for the gifts: namely, the edification of the Body of Christ (1 Corinthians 12:7). One would be hard-pressed to conclude that the church is no longer in need of edification, and therefore beyond the need of Christians empowered by God's Spirit with unique gifts meant to build up and strengthen His Body.

The Functional Cessationist would hold that the purpose of the sign-gifts of speaking in tongues and miraculous healing most notably authenticated the Apostles (Acts 5:15, 19:12), yet there is no reason to believe that these gifts have ceased today (John 14:12–14; 1 Corinthians 12:31,14:1–18). Furthermore, Functional Cessationism holds that although the Bible is God's only trustworthy voice, believers should "let the Holy Spirit guide our lives" (Galatians 5:16) and leave room within the traditionally held Western Enlightenment worldview that tends to create a wall between the experiential framework of the senses and the supernatural framework of the biblical authors.[38] In other words, when guided by the Bible, believers have more to gain than lose in opening their mind to the idea that the same Holy Spirit who acted supernaturally in the lives of the Apostles and early church is active and alive in similar ways today.

At the other end of the spectrum, many notable theologians believe in Cessationism and that the diffusion of miraculous gifts by the Holy Spirit was confined to the apostolic church and subsequently passed away with it.[39] Because abuses and exaggerations of continuing miraculous experiences with the Holy Spirit are so rampant and abusive in the church, it is better to rely solely on the revealed wisdom of the Bible.[40] Although the Cessationist view contends that the miraculous gifts were reserved for the Apostles and served the purpose of

---

[37] Sam Storms, *Practicing the Power* (Grand Rapids, MI: Zondervan, 2017), p. 246.
[38] Tennent, p. 178.
[39] B. B. Warfield in his book *Counterfeit Miracles* as identified in Christian Theology, p. 172.
[40] Breshears, Western Seminary TH503 outline on Holy Spirit

establishing the church, it is important to note that numerous non-apostolic men and women exercised these gifts including the 70 who were commissioned in Luke 10:9 and at least 108 of the 120 who were gathered in the upper room on the day of Pentecost. Furthermore, the Cessationist's appeal to Ephesians 2:20 that the gifts were for the first century period of time in which the church was being built overlooks the fact that miraculous gifts (specifically the gift of prophecy) were not linked to the apostles and never functioned foundationally.[41]

Theologian Millard Erickson argues for what appears to be a Cessationist view and suggests that even if the Spirit were to actively dispense special gifts in the church today, Christians "are not to set their lives to seeking them." Erickson points to Paul's teaching that the Spirit dispenses the gifts sovereignly, and that He alone will determine the recipients (1 Corinthians 12:11). This being the case, the Spirit may choose to give a believer a special gift regardless of their prayers or expectation of it. Erickson reiterates the fact that Paul's command to be "filled with the Spirit" (Ephesians 5:18) is a *present imperative*, which suggests an ongoing action and experience in the daily life of the believer.

A careful assessment of the totality of the positions (with a special emphasis on the points I feel were unfairly made by Erickson) compels me to lean toward a Continuationism theology. Although I certainly agree with Erickson's view of the sovereignty of the Spirit, it is supremely important to note that according to Paul, in the particular case of miraculous gifts, the Spirit can be quenched (1 Thessalonians 5:19–22). This is a remarkable thought considering that Paul is speaking about the sovereign Spirit of God who works all things together according to His will. Nevertheless, here Paul warns believers that God has granted Christians the ability to either "*restrict or release* what He does in the life of the local church."[42] Furthermore, in 1 Corinthians 14:32, Paul explains, "The spirits of prophets are subject to prophets." This means that the Spirit is happy to align Himself with the believer's expectations for what is possible, and will "not act upon us or through us as if we were puppets."[43] This line

---

[41] Storms, p. 249.
[42] Storms, p. 180.
[43] Storms, p. 180.

of reasoning seems to contradict Erickson and suggests that believers have a responsibility to not just seek the Spirit—but so much of Him that we "fan the flame of the Spirit's fire" (2 Timothy 1:6).

Perhaps the most compelling reason to embrace the active pursuit of the Spirit is our Lord's teaching on the subject. In Luke 11:13, in the context of explaining the magnitude of God's grace, Jesus said, "If you then, who are evil, know how to give good gifts to your children, *how much more will the heavenly Father give the Holy Spirit to those who ask him*" (Luke 11:13—my emphasis). In application within the believer's life, we have the confidence that God intimately knows our every need and is fully aware of the emptiness in our life. This means that on one hand God knows what we need even before we ask for it, and on the other hand God wants us to ask (Matthew 7:7–11). Weighing all the evidence—with special attention given to our Lord's discourse—leads me to believe that God is far more willing to fill us with His Spirit than we are willing to ask.

EXERCISING OUR FAITH

I BELIVE THAT ALL OF the gifts of the Spirit continue to be given by God to believers today and are fully operative in the Body of Christ. These gifts may be immediately accompanied by the initial conversion experience; or similar to the way that a physical muscle grows stronger over time, the gifts may develop gradually throughout the believer's lifetime. This being said, I must emphasize the fact that I believe the Holy Spirit indwells believers at the moment of their conversion. The question we may very well consider at this point is what should be expected in the life of the believer *following their conversion*? The answer could not be any clearer—the Bible plainly teaches that following the initial conversion experience and the receipt of the Holy Spirit, the believer is called to a life of increasing sanctification and growing in Christlikeness (2 Thessalonians 2:13; Colossians 3:1, 5). Fundamentally, I believe this means that although the Holy Spirit comes to indwell every person at conversion, there is an ongoing experience throughout the believer's new life in Christ of being continually *filled with the Spirit*.

By way of illustration, consider an athlete who enrolls into a CrossFit gym. The moment of conversion takes place during their initial entry and enrollment into the fitness studio. However, the real benefits to the athlete of the program are derived from the daily experience of applying the methodology of constantly varied, functional movement, at high intensity. Some athletes might enjoy rather sudden "breakthroughs" in advanced gymnastic movements or weightlifting skills, whereas others tend to need more time to see any evidence of growth. But in either case, the increase in strength (to borrow theological language—*filling the muscles*) is clearly subsequent to, and a secondary effect of, the initial entry into the gym.

Pressing this illustration into the context of the church, the subsequent filling with the Spirit may be gradual or rather dramatic (1 Corinthians 12:7–11), and occurs as a result of living out the reality of being baptized by the Spirit.[44] This perpetual filling is not to be confused with a distinct second blessing of the Holy Spirit, but rather "an actualization of what we have already received at conversion."[45] This conclusion, however, brings us to face to face with very two very interesting and compelling questions: Should the believer actively pray for, seek out, and make room for the ongoing filling of the Spirit? And if so, what are the functional steps a believer should take in pursuit of an encounter with the Spirit? Returning for a moment to our CrossFit analogy, the athlete desirous of increasing in strength will take great measures to create the appropriate environment in their life to facilitate such growth. Should Christians model and adopt such athletic behavior into our spiritual life?

---

[44] Breshears, Western Seminary TH503 outline on Holy Spirit.
[45] Breshears, Western Seminary TH503 outline on Holy Spirit.

THE IMPLICATIONS OF THE EASTER INBREATHING

THE APOSTLE JOHN RECORDS A meeting that Jesus had with his disciples that is sometimes referred to as the "Easter Inbreathing." After appearing to His disciples in His resurrected body and showing them His hands and side, Jesus said, "'Peace be with you. As the Father has sent me, even so I am sending you.' And when He had said this, He breathed on them and said to them, 'Receive the Holy Spirit'" (John 20:21–22).[46] It is important to note that although Jesus gave the disciples the Holy Spirit on this particular day, He still commanded them to wait for a secondary experience that would take place when they would be "baptized with the Holy Spirit" (Acts 1:4–5). How can we reconcile what appears to be two distinct baptisms?

I believe that the 11 disciples who were breathed on by Jesus are the archetype of Christians today who receive the Holy Spirit at conversion but remain idle (or even worse, powerless) *to witness their faith*. Although the 11 disciples initially received the Holy Spirit on the Easter Inbreathing, they were filled with the Spirit on the Day of Pentecost. It this sense, it was the second experience with the Holy Spirit that led to a "life-changing encounter that forever transformed them, turning ordinary men into firebrands for God, willing to face harsh criticism, beatings, and dying for the cause of Christ."[47] To recapitulate the series of events, when Jesus met with the disciples behind closed doors, breathed on them, and commanded them to receive the Holy Spirit, they received the Spirit of God in that very moment—representative of the experience believers have today when they first put their faith in Christ. However, when the 11 disciples were baptized by the Holy Spirit on the Day of Pentecost, they had a face-to-face encounter with the Holy Spirit that completely transformed their lives. This being the case, believers today have much to learn from those who *waited for the gift the Father promised.*

---

[46] In the context of our Lord's command to "Receive the Holy Spirit," in *A Manual Grammar of the Greek New Testament*, H. E. Dana points out that Jesus used an aorist tense, the meaning of which is "right now!" In other words, the giving of the Holy Spirit took place immediately, and should not be confused with the idea that Jesus was speaking to a future event. H. E. Dana, *A Manual Grammar of the Greek New Testament* (New York, NY: Macmillan Publishers, 1957), p. 300.
[47] Sala, p. 108.

APPLICATION IN THE BOX

JESUS MADE IT CLEAR TO his disciples that there must be a "hunger and thirst for God" before that desire can be fulfilled. To this effect, the Apostle John elaborated on our Lord's teaching on the Holy Spirit by recording: "On the last day of the feast, the *great day*, Jesus stood up and cried out, 'If anyone thirsts, let him come to me and drink. Whoever believes in me, as the Scripture has said, out of his heart will flow rivers of living water'" (John 7:37–38). Christians alive today inhabit the world of the feast—the great day in which our Lord's Spirit will be poured out into those who believe (John 7:38–40). This means that believers must have an active and conscious desire for the Holy Spirit, while also praying that "the Spirit would have full control over the will, emotions, and reasoning faculties of the believer."[48]

As a simple illustration from the CrossFit studio, in over 20 years of coaching athletes to achieve their first muscle-up, I have noticed a curious thing. Athletes who had a "hunger and thirst" for their first muscle-up (a very challenging gymnastic movement performed on the high-rings) achieved it in record time compared with people who thought it would never happen. In this sense, I propose there is an intimate connection between obedience, waiting on the Lord, and positive expectancy on the gift of the Holy Spirit. Acts 5:32 speaks of the Spirit "whom God has given to *those who obey Him*."[49] This magnificent verse testifies to the great truth that believers can experience more of the Spirit, not based on anything that we do, but rather on the type of people that we are. Are we obedient? Do we have faith? Do we wait on our Lord?

Following our Lords command to *patiently wait* on the gift promised by the Father (Acts 1:4), Jesus's last words to His disciples were, "But you will receive power when the Holy Spirit has come upon you, and you will be my witness in Jerusalem and in all Judea and Samaria, and to the ends of

---

[48] Kenneth Wuest, "The Holy Spirit in Greek Exposition," *Bibliotheca Sacra*, CXIIX. Quoted in Dr. Harold Sala's book, *Getting Acquainted with the Holy Spirit*, p. 119.
[49] My use of italics in this verse to emphasize obedience to the Lord resulted in the gift of the Holy Spirit.

the earth" (Acts 1:8–9). Whereas a great many people in the church today are quite content to be an *advocate* of the Christian faith, it seems that very few are actively *witnessing* their faith to the extent that we read about in the New Testament. Therefore, let us note three characteristics of a true *Christian witness* and how they affect our pursuit of the spiritual gifts.

In a court of law, a witness testifies on their first-hand knowledge of an experience. In order for something to be admitted as actual evidence (as opposed to hearsay or mere speculation), the witness must be able to declare, "*I know* this to be true" rather than "I *think* this is true." Second, a real witness is not of words, but of deeds (James 2:14–26). Peter and John astonished the Sanhedrin because of their courage (Acts 4:13). In other words, it was *who they were that was significant*, which led the inquisitors to conclude: "These men had been with Jesus" (Acts 4:13b). New Testament scholar William Barclay relates a story in which journalist Sir Henry Morton Stanley, having spent time with evangelist David Livingstone in central Africa, said: "If I had been with him any longer, I would have been compelled to be a Christian—and he never spoke to me about it at all." And perhaps most importantly, the Greek word for *witness* and the word for *martyr* is the same (martus). To be a witness means to be loyal to the faith—no matter the cost.[50]

The world that Christians inhabit today moves at an extremely fast pace. In a fiber-optic Internet cable, the speed at which a data packet can travel is nearly 200,000 kilometers per second, (or 124,300 miles per second).[51] Considering the circumference of Earth is about 40,000 kilometers, this is *mind-boggling* fast. Caught up in the speed of the world around us, is it possible that a believer's expectation for an immediate life-changing encounter with the Holy Spirit at the moment of conversion—or at a time subsequent to conversion—has been unfairly swayed by common culture? In the context of the CrossFit Box, the most discouraging reality athletes must face is the fact that fitness goals often

---

[50] The three qualities of a "Christian Witness" were brought to my attention William Barclay's *The Acts of the Apostles Daily Study Bible* (Louisville, KY: Westminster John Knox Press, 2017), p. 13.

[51] NetworkingGuides.com.

take a very long time to achieve. In many cases, I have discovered that unless athletes are able to experience near immediate evidence of progress, it can be difficult for them to sustain the necessary momentum to eventually achieve— and perhaps even surpass—what they think is possible. In this sense, what is the capacity for a believer today to wait an indefinite period of time for either a distinct second encounter, or a more gradual filling, of the Holy Spirit? And is the principle and expectation of waiting even biblical?

Moving our illustrations of waiting from the CrossFit Box to the Body of Christ, believers must hold within their mind two seemingly conflicting ideas. On one hand, it is important to note that in the New Testament, the coming of the Spirit is the fulfillment of the promise of Jesus: "And remember, I am with you always, to the end of the age" (Matthew 28:20). This means that at the moment of conversion, Jesus is with us through His Spirit, and in this sense there is no waiting at all. On the other hand, in Acts 1:4, the apostles are specifically commanded to *wait for the coming of the Spirit*. How are we to reconcile what appears to be a "now—then" reality?

I believe that Christians would gain more power and confidence to witness their faith if they followed the example of the apostles and learned to wait for the Lord. In other words, Christians today (in particular Christian athletes within the CrossFit culture) need to develop *skillfulness in stillness*. Amid a world of hurry-up and get things done, we must cultivate space in our heart to slow down and receive. Given that everything about the sport of CrossFit revolves around the principle of *doing more work in less time*, the prophet Isaiah's words are more applicable today than ever before: "Those who wait for the Lord shall renew their strength" (Isaiah 40:31).

In his book *Baptism and Fullness*, author John Stott relates, "The baptism was a unique initiatory experience; the fullness was intended to be the continuing, the permanent result, the norm. As an initiatory event the baptism is not repeatable and cannot be lost, but the fullness can be repeated and in any case needs to be maintained."[52]

---

[52] John Stott, *Baptism and Fullness* (Downers Grove, IL: InterVarsity Press, 1964), p. 62.

When I first started in CrossFit in December 2001, the program's founder told me that I should look forward to 20 years of favorable athletic adaptation and steady physical development. Reflecting on the past 20 years of CrossFit training, my increasingly high stack of fitness journals is evidence of the resounding truth of the founder's statement. I can't help but conclude that the relationship between my subjective thoughts and expectations about my progress, and the actual objective measurement of my progress, were intimately connected. In other words, I have a strong sense that my physical progress and growth in the program are directly attributed to my expectations about the possibility for such growth in the first place. Succinctly stated, the thought preceded (and arguably produced) the outcome.

Against this background, it is interesting to note the role of faith in receiving a subsequent encounter with the Holy Spirit following conversion. I find that I must differentiate between different types of faith in order to make this point. All believers exercise the first type of faith, which I refer to as *converting faith*— this faith takes place at the moment of our conversion, and is present in every born-again believer. The second type of faith is a *continuing faith*, which is that daily confidence that God is with us, and that He will never leave or forsake us (Deuteronomy 31:6). In biblical-historical context, Abraham demonstrated *converting faith* when he "obeyed when God called him to leave home and go to another land" (Hebrews 11:8a), and *continuing faith* when he pressed forward each day "without knowing where he was going" (Hebrews 11:8b).

In addition to *converting* and *continuing faith*, I also believe there is a third type of faith that author and pastor Sam Storms has defined as *charismatic faith*, which is a "sudden, supernatural surge of confident assurance that God is going to do something right now, right here."[53] To this effect, it is interesting to note that when Jesus returned to His hometown of Nazareth, He was only able to accomplish a few miracles there because of the people's lack of faith (or perhaps *charismatic faith*?—Matthew 13:54–58). On the other hand, in instances of

---

[53] Storms, p. 53. The distinctions between, "Three Types of Faith" were brought to my attention by Storm's section on "The Role of Faith" in his masterful book, *Practicing the Power.*

Jesus healing people, it was commonly accompanied by the fact that they had faith in Him (Luke 7:50, 8:48, 18:42). Given the relationship between faith and healing, it would seem that faith in God's ability to enable a distinct encounter with Him might very well be largely in the hands (or head) of the believer.

It is also important to remember that Paul wrote, "The spirits of prophets are subject to prophets" (1 Corinthians 14:32). Paul's point is that the Holy Spirit does not move through believers as if we were mindless sedentary beings. Rather, the "sovereign Spirit happily subjects Himself to our decisions."[54] In other words, believers who hold in their theological framework the idea that a distinct experience with the Holy Spirit is possible are far more likely to have their expectations and prayers met than someone who believes it's just not going to happen.

Legendary Drug Enforcement Administration (DEA) supervisory Special Agent and Firearms Instructor John Browning told my investigative group, "It's better to have a back-up gun and not need it, then need a back-up gun, and not have one." In the perilous moment that a Law Enforcement Officer finds himself in need of a back-up gun, it means that something has gone horribly amiss, and lives are on the line. Pressing the street-savvy wisdom of Agent Browning into a theological construct, we may very well conclude that it's far better to believe that a powerful encounter with the Holy Spirit is possible after conversion and not experience it during our lifetime—than to discover in the afterlife that while on earth the Holy Spirit was desirous of uniquely empowering us to edify the Body of Christ—yet sadly we never thought to ask.

---

[54] Storms, p. 180.

HOLD ON A MINUTE —
WHAT ABOUT SPEAKING IN TONGUES?

IN SOME PENTECOSTAL AND CHARISMATIC denominations, a theology gradually developed that taught absent the spiritual gift of speaking in tongues, a believer has not been baptized in the Holy Spirit. This doctrine is based primarily on the fact that speaking in tongues was often accompanied by the outpouring of the Holy Spirit (Acts 2:4, 10:46, 19:6). From this reasoning, one could easily conclude that the outpouring of the Spirit and speaking in tongues should constitute a normal and anticipated experience for everyone. However, this conclusion tragically overlooks the fact that this would mean that anyone who does not speak in tongues is not Spirit-filled—a concept that is clearly not in alignment with the biblical teaching of baptism (1 Corinthians 12:27–31). Furthermore, this position would put a great number of renowned men of God in the category of "not Spirit-filled" including Billy Graham and Charles Spurgeon.[55]

When Paul addressed the matter of speaking in tongues, he asked the question, "Do all speak in tongues?" (1 Corinthians 12:30). As renowned New Testament scholar Harold Sala has pointed out in his book, *Getting Acquainted with the Holy Spirit*, in the Greek language a question can be asked in such a way that the speaker makes it clear that either a "Yes" or a "No" is expected. In the case of the question asked by Paul, the expected answer is "No!"[56] I must reiterate at this point that I do not mean to imply that tongues have ceased, or that a believer and should not actively pray for or exercise this particular gift. Rather, I humbly suggest that the Body of Christ must be careful not to overemphasize the gift of tongues or require it as demonstrable proof of a Spirit-filled life.

God knows His children better than we know ourselves, and when we invite Him to be Lord over our life, our encounter with Him will be as completely unique as the individual believer himself.

YES and AMEN.

---

[55] Sala, p. 133.
[56] Sala, p. 134.

LESSON ELEVEN

THE STONES OF OUR FAITH

LESSON ELEVEN
THE STONES OF OUR FAITH

THE WORD OF GOD:

Then David took his staff in his hand, chose five smooth stones from the stream, and put them in the pouch of his shepherd's bag and, with his sling in his hand, approached the Philistine.

(1 Samuel 17:40)

MY BROTHERS AND MY SISTERS, may the grace of our Lord Jesus Christ, the love of God, and the fellowship of the Holy Spirit, be with you (2 Corinthians 13:14). I want to study with you today the awesome topic of *The Stones of Our Faith*. It never ceases to amaze me how often I return to the epic story of David and Goliath. It seems that each time I do, I discover something "new and wonderful" in God's Word (reference Psalm 119:18). Let's revisit this familiar story with a sense of adventure and joyful expectancy for the transformational power of Holy Scripture.

....

A YOUNG MAN LOOKS DOWN into a stream of clear water at the very bottom of a valley. Above him on the hilltop stood two opposing armies. At the highest point on the landscape, having already captured the coveted terrain feature of the high ground, loomed a fearsome giant, covered head to toe in bronze armor, holding a sword nearly the length of a grown man's body.

If this young man had taken the time to study the reflection of his image in the stream, he would have seen a handsome face, slightly sunburned from long hours of being outdoors in the sun. Described by a friend as "strong, handsome, courageous, and well spoken" (1 Samuel 16:8), this young man was respected as being a hard worker and loyal to his craft.

However, this young man had not come to the stream to look at his face in the water. He had come to look for stones. Five smooth stones, to be exact. You see, this young man was looking for a particularly smooth, flat stone that would sit perfectly in the leather strap of his shepherd's sling. He had already used the sling to great effect, having killed a lion and a bear that once threatened his flock. However, his target today would walk on two feet, instead of four, and was tormenting not sheep but rather the army of Israel, and had been for forty days, and forty nights. This young man had come to fight a giant. Perhaps you have heard his name before—I am speaking of none other than David, the mighty man after God's own heart.

Goliath blatantly strutted in the distance, a formidable foe. In fact, not a single man had dared to step forward to face him in combat. King Saul, the appointed king of the army of Israel, was for all intents and purposes responsible for engaging the enemy. However, even the king remained hidden away within the refuge of his tent. If Goliath had looked and seen David, alone there by the creek, he would surely have laughed at the prospect of any outcome other than the small man's death by the hand of his sword. Goliath was a big man. Scripture says he stood 9 feet, 9 inches tall, and carried 160 pounds of armor. And, to make matters worse, Goliath relentlessly provoked the army with the words, "This day I defy the ranks of Israel, give me a man and let us fight each other" (1 Samuel 17:8). But nobody showed up. In fact, those on the battlefield had turned and run the other direction.

That is, everyone but David. Which begs the question: What was David doing on the battlefield? After all, he was not enlisted in the army. He'd never been trained in military maneuvers, and although he had fought and killed predatory animals, he had never faced a giant. The Scripture reveals that David had been sent by his father to bring bread to his brothers. You see, David's brothers were in the army, and David had come to bring them the fellowship of a family meal.

HOW TO GO UP IN LIFE

THE FIRST POINT I WANT to emphasize in this lesson is the supremacy of God's grace. God's grace is everywhere you look in the Scriptures—you just need to have the spiritual key to unlock and discover what might have otherwise remained buried in the sands of an ancient battlefield. Did you know that Jesus said that all the Scriptures were about Himself? In explaining the purpose of studying the Scriptures to a group of his disciples, Jesus said, "the Scriptures testify about me" (John 5:39).

On another occasion, Jesus said, "everything must be fulfilled that is written about me that is written in the book of Moses, the Prophets and the Psalms" (Luke 24:44). This means that in some way, shape, or form, our task whenever we study the Bible is to look for Jesus. This also means that as we recall the familiar story of David and Goliath, we must discipline ourselves to see it not with the eyes in our head, but rather the eyes in our heart.

Grace is described in the Bible as underserved. Freely given. A gift from a loving God. The Apostle Paul provides a litmus test for grace—there is nothing you can do to earn it, and you can't claim any responsibility for having received it. In other words, you can't brag about grace. And we see it here on the battlefield. David, as a symbol of a loving father's grace, brings his brothers a meal. And not just any meal—bread, to be exact. When we remember in the New Testament that Jesus referred to himself as the bread of life, immediately the connection is made. David's brothers were marked for death that fateful day, as was everyone else in King Saul's army. This means that Goliath represents the enemy of sin and death, and when David came onto the scene, he took the place of his brother and fought the battle for them. There needed to be what is referred to in the military as a "change of command." David was that change, and he brought with him not only lunch, but also life. This is exactly what Jesus does in your life, my friends.

As we study the Scriptures and imagine this particular scene, it's interesting to access the terrain features of the ancient battlefield. In the days of close combat, when the tip of a spear and the edge of a sword settled battles, the opponent who secured the high ground had a decisive advantage. And the high ground was precisely the terrain that Goliath had claimed. This means that the enemy had the highest terrain, whereas David had seemingly retreated to the lowest. You see, the stream that David went to in search of five smooth stones was, geographically speaking, the lowest place you could go.

THE FOUNDATION OF YOUR FAITH

THIS LEADS US TO THE second point of today's study: If you want to go up in life, you first need to go down. James, the half-brother of Jesus, wrote, "humble yourself before the Lord, and he will lift you up" (James 4:10). The temptation we all have whenever we face a giant—whether it is the giant of a job loss, a career change, the breakup of a relationship, or the anxiety caused by the effects of a disease—is to access the giant according to our own strength. We ask ourselves, "How am I going to face this giant?" That, my friend, is entirely the wrong question to ask. It's not the size of the giant that matters, it's the size of our God. Well, you might ask yourself, "There certainly must be something that I need to do. What is my responsibility in the battle? What is my share of the work?" To answer this, we need only look to the words of Jesus, who said, "The work of God is this: to believe in the one he has sent" (John 6:29).

Now, I know that's challenging to do! Part of us always feels like we need to do something, and it's always a double-edged sword. Either I'm not capable of doing what I think needs to be done, or I do something that only complicates the problem and makes matters worse. Did you know that in the context of our story, David's own brothers did not believe in the one whom their father had sent? In fact, they ridiculed David and said that he had no part in the battle. Even James, Jesus Christ's own brother, didn't believe that Jesus was sent from the Father until James saw Jesus after the resurrection. Then he humbled himself, and, from that day forward, referred to himself as "a servant of God and of the Lord Jesus Christ" (James 1:1). The Bible declares that God wants to fight your battles for you, and that you only need to be still. In this stillness, there is humbleness and faithfulness in the goodness of God.

The third and final point I want to emphasize is the importance of establishing the foundation of your faith. To help set the proper context for the importance of what I want to share with you, imagine this scenario: an active shooter has just walked onto an elementary school campus. Immediately, a 911 call goes out, and a fraction of a second later, the dispatch center alerts a police officer on patrol less than a block away. However, rather than immediately responding to the school, the officer drives in the other direction! They head to a local sporting goods store to purchase ammunition for their firearm. Although they were on active criminal patrol and were wearing their uniform, complete with a duty belt, handgun, and even extra magazines, they did not have a single round of ammunition anywhere on their person. Well, clearly, this just doesn't make sense. And in the context of our biblical story, it doesn't make any sense that David would arrive on the battlefield carrying his sling (the equivalent of a firearm) with his shepherd's pouch (the equivalent of a magazine pouch) without a single stone (the equivalent of a round of ammunition).

Therefore, when David retreated down the valley to the stream to gather five smooth stones, the stones appear to represent more than just physical objects. I think God wants us to see something more important. I propose that David already had plenty of ammunition stored in his pouch. What David wanted and needed on that fateful day is the same thing that you and I need today: a moment of reprieve from the intensity of the battle. David needed a moment of silence, and solitude, and peace in the presence of God in order to remind himself of all the ways that God had blessed his life. And this is exactly the same thing we need—in the intensity, complexity, uncertainty, and difficulty of our days, we need to humble ourselves before God and remind ourselves of his goodness. Here is the key to understanding this ancient story: *before David faced his giant, he needed to face his God.* And before you face your giants, you first need to face your God.

I propose that symbolically, each of the five stones represents one of the foundations to our faith. A wonderful spiritual exercise is to reflect on the "stones of your faith." Based on what we know about David, I'll share with you five compelling stones to store in your shepherd's pouch. To make these stones easy to remember, they all begin with the letter "P."

1) The stone of prayer (Go down before you go up!)
2) The stone of persistence (David was prepared for multiple opponents!)
3) The stone of priority (Only David talked about God!)
4) The stone of positive expectancy (David talked about victory!)
5) The stone of physical training (David was strong!)

Let's begin with the stone of prayer. In the context of CrossFit, if you want to lift a barbell *upward*, you need to apply force *downward*. Although it seems counterintuitive, the fact remains that the degree of force you can apply downward against the earth has a direct effect on the amount of power you are able to generate upward on the barbell. This being the case, why would we think it would be anything different in the spiritual ordering of things? David knew that the key to overcoming the challenges that he faced in life was through prayer and intimate fellowship with God.

David also knew that sometimes it took more than one prayer to defeat a giant. In this sense, the second stone speaks to the importance of persistence in your prayer life. Furthermore, whether you like it or not, everything in your life has been achieved (either intentionally or unintentionally) through the power of persistence. In any given moment of your life, you have an opportunity to take an inventory of everything that you are grateful for and then to identify the variable that you had persistently practiced in order to bring your goals to fruition. On the other hand, if there are things in your life that you do not want to carry with you into the next season, you can identity the associated variable and stop doing it!

The third stone addresses the principle of "putting first things first." Whereas everyone else on the battlefield was focused on the giant, David was focused on God. In fact, it's all that David could talk about! In 1 Samuel 17 (the chapter in the Bible that records David and Goliath), it is incredible to see that David spoke about God on nine different occasions, compared to the two mentions that David made of Goliath. And based on the stone of positive expectancy, it is no wonder that when David did speak about Goliath, it was in the context of defeating him in battle! As one of my mentors used to constantly remind me, "You need to make God your first priority, and not your last resort."

The fourth stone serves to remind us of the awesome power of our expectations. By a mysterious law of creation, we tend to move in the direction of the thoughts and expectations we have for ourselves, for each other, and for God. It's interesting to note that in the context of David and Goliath, whereas everyone else on the battlefield was *expecting defeat*, David was *expecting victory* (reference 1 Samuel 17:24–26). David was so certain that he would defeat Goliath that he was already thinking about the reward "for the man who kills this Philistine and removes this disgrace from Israel" (1 Samuel 17:25–26). Reasoning from this fact, it is exceedingly important for you to remain positive in both your speaking and thinking. An outstanding Bible verse that reiterates this is Proverbs 4:23: "Above all else guard your heart, for everything you do flows from it." If you recall from Lesson 5, in the Bible, the heart is the seat of human will; thus, the heart is the central and unifying organ of our personal life. When our deepest and innermost thoughts (our heart) are absolutely convinced of the goodness of God, then a sense of positive expectancy about every season of life is the natural result.

The fifth and final stone reminds us of the importance of physical training and proper care of our body. Your body is the temple of the Holy Spirit and the instrument by which God can work in and through your life. The incarnation means that God took upon Himself a human body to live in and work through. In Paul's Letter to the Romans, he wrote, "present your bodies to God" (Romans 12:1). In historical context, this was an astonishing thing to say! To the Greeks, what mattered was the spirit; the body was only a prison house, something to be despised and even ashamed of. However, in Paul's theology of the human body, he taught that a Christian's body was just as important to God as was their soul, mind, and spirit. This means that we can serve God through the totality of our human makeup. Reasoning from this fact, a strong physical body can be an instrument in the service of God's Kingdom. In other words, your daily workout can be worship!

CONCLUDING THOUGHTS

IN CONCLUDING THIS LESSON, I would be amiss if I did not mention David's complete reliance on the strength of God. Everyone on the battlefield that fateful day looked at Goliath and observed an *impossible situation*. However, David looked at God and believed that God could make *the impossible entirely possible*. This means that as long as you go through life thinking that everything depends on your own effort, you are bound to be a pessimist and will tend to gravitate toward a negative outlook on every challenge you face. On the other hand, when you realize that it is never about your own effort—but rather it is always God's grace and power that matter, then you become an optimist. Like David, you embrace a faith that proclaims, "With God on my side, all things are possible."

And to this I say,

YES and AMEN.

LESSON TWELVE

THE SUPREMACY OF GOD'S GRACE

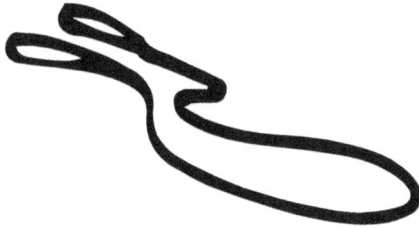

LESSON TWELVE
THE SUPREMACY OF GOD'S GRACE

THE WORD OF GOD:

The next day, John was there again with two of his disciples. When he saw Jesus passing by, he said, "Look, the Lamb of God!"

When the two disciples heard him say this, they followed Jesus. Turning around, Jesus saw them following him and asked, "What do you want?"

They said "Rabbi" (which means "Teacher"), "where are you staying?"

"Come," he replied, "and you will see."

(John 1:35–39)

MY BROTHERS AND MY SISTERS, may the grace of our Lord Jesus Christ, the love of God, and the fellowship of the Holy Spirit be with you (2 Corinthians 13:14). I want to study with you today the awesome topic of *The Supremacy of God's Grace*. This being the twelfth and final lesson of this book, I thought it would be fitting to embrace the principle of *virtuosity* in our Gospel reading by "reviewing the basics." Although we studied John 1:35–41 in Lesson Four, I feel that we need to revisit the astonishing revelation of God's grace contained within these few verses (specifically 1:35–39). I am so encouraged by the incredible touch of God's grace found within this short passage of Scripture. Although it is only four verses, I promise that we shall soon discover a deep reservoir of spiritual wisdom, revelation, and knowledge that will fill your heart with joy. In the words of the great biblical scholar William Barclay, "Never was a passage of scripture fuller of more important revealing touches than this."

Let's begin by noticing the prominent figure of John the Baptist. Characteristic of John was his humbleness before the Lord and his desire to point people beyond himself. Have you noticed how easy it is to point people to yourself? We seem to be hardwired to desire attention, accolade, acclaim, and the acknowledgment of others. However, John teaches us that there is another way of abiding in the world, and that is to take the attention off ourselves and put it onto God. This was the pattern of all the great saints of the Bible. In one way or another, Abraham, Daniel, Moses, and David—all those who were called friends of the

Lord—had the uncanny ability and meekness of heart to freely recognize their own shortcomings. However, in their weakness was their strength, for God Almighty was able to freely work through the conduit of His children.

Perhaps one reason that we are fearful of turning attention away from ourselves is that we are jealous of others and—maybe at a level so deep it only influences the subconscious mind—we are jealous of God. The root of all sin is idolatry, which is turning something other than God into God. Very often, the god we worship is the god of our own pride, acclaim, popularity, and social status. This is one reason that I love and admire John the Baptist. He must have known very well that to speak to his disciples about Jesus the way that he did was to invite them to leave him and transfer their loyalty to this new and greater teacher. Yet he still did it. There was not a single ounce of jealousy in John. He had come to lead other people to Christ, not to himself. There is no harder task than to freely surrender to second place; nevertheless, as soon as Jesus emerged on the scene, John never had any other thought than to send people to him.

This being the case, did you notice to whom John sent his disciples? "The Lamb of God" meant only one thing—this story would not end well for the disciples. Jewish people were all too familiar with the implications of the sacrificial lamb—it was put to death as atonement for the sins of the people. This means that when we follow Jesus, we must be prepared to take up our cross and to follow Him even when the road becomes rough. I recall one of my Army instructors chiding me and saying, "Everyone wants to be in the Army on a bright sunny day!" The funny thing is, in twelve years of military service, I recall only a handful of sunny (let alone bright) days. Rather, they were filled with stormy weather and were in uncomfortable environments and conditions that I would have rather done without.

Surely the disciples knew what they were in for. Reasoning from this fact, although they had left John to follow Jesus, perhaps they were a bit timid and followed from a respectful and uncertain distance. Maybe they were shy. We could even imagine that they were afraid. In the traditional spiritual path of other world religions, it is the devotees who follow after their guru. In this sense, the text for a moment seems to suggest that a similar series of events is now taking place in the lives of the two disciples. But then Jesus did something that is both radical and entirely characteristic of God. He turned and spoke to them. That is to say, Jesus met them halfway. He made things easier for them. He opened the door so that they might come in. He invited them into His life.

This is what Jesus does when He comes into your life. He opens your eyes and enables you to see things that you never saw before. He turns you from darkness to light. Before people enter into a relationship with Jesus, they are essentially walking in the wrong direction, immersed in a life of sin. It's interesting that the Aramaic word for sin that Jesus used, *Kata*, was an ancient archery term that meant three things: to miss the target, to fall short of the target, or to shoot the arrow in the entirely wrong direction. In either event, when Jesus comes into your life, He forgives your sins. Your past is forgiven and, for the future, your life is re-created and purified—what we refer to in theology as increasingly sanctified and comforted to His image.

We also see in Jesus' actions a symbol of the divine initiative of God's grace. It is always God who takes the first step. The moment that our thoughts go to God, and our heart reaches out to Him, God comes to meet us far more than just halfway. God will never leave a man or woman to search and search after Him. Rather, God goes out to meet you wherever you are. The great theologian and early Church Father Augustine said, "We could not even have begun to seek God unless He had already found us." This means that when we go to God, we do not go in vain. Nor are we dependent on the work of our hands, the intellect of our mind, or the capacity of our heart to enjoy fellowship with Him. Rather, by grace through faith, God enters our life and transforms us into the image of His Son.

Jesus began by asking these two men the most fundamental question in life: "What do you want?" In Greek, the word that Jesus used was *Zeter*, which means "to seek after or to strive for." In other words, Jesus asked, "What are you seeking?" It's interesting to note that in other world religions, it was the common practice of the devotee to ask the guru a question. However, here we see something entirely different, yet at the same time so beautifully characteristic of God. After all, in the creation account of Genesis, God asked Adam (Hebrew for "mankind") two illuminating questions: "Where are you?" (Genesis 13:9) and "Who told you that?" (Genesis 13:11). Consider how this "trifecta" of questions impacts your life today. The question "Where are you?" speaks to your physical nature and everything that makes up the material existence of your daily life.

The question "Who told you that?" speaks to your innermost thoughts—the way that you think about yourself, about other people, and, most importantly, about God. A. W. Tozer said, "The thoughts that come into your mind about God are the most important thoughts about you." And finally, "What do you want? What are you searching for? What are you seeking, and striving after?"

WHAT DO YOU WANT?

IT WOULD BE WELL WITH US if every now and again we were to ask ourselves all three of these profound questions. However, for our purposes within this lesson, let's contemplate for a moment the implications of the question that Jesus asked His disciples, "What are you looking for? What is your aim and goal? What do you really want to get out of life?"

Perhaps some of you are searching for security. You would like a position in life that is safe and provides enough money to meet the needs of life, plus a little left over for material comforts. This is not a wrong aim, but it is a low aim and an inadequate thing in which to direct all of your life energy. As our world has painfully witnessed, there is no safe security in the changing tides of life. In the final analysis, we leave everything behind and take nothing with us. This is akin to our arrow falling short of the target.

So, perhaps we aim higher. Maybe you are searching for a career, or purpose, meaning, and mission in life. If this motive is in service of others, then indeed the arrow may very well now be on target but still miss the mark—you've not yet hit the bull's-eye.

What, then, are we searching for? What is the right answer? Perhaps when it is all boiled down, we are all searching for the same thing. In this sense, we are truly brothers and sisters, of the same family. Could it be that we are all searching for some kind of peace? Are we all searching for something to enable us to be at peace with ourselves, with each other, and, most importantly, with God? I propose that in our heart of hearts, this is what we all want, and this is why, to a greater or lesser degree, we all want (and desperately need) God.

So what did the disciples of John say to Jesus? What was it they were searching for? It is interesting that according to our Gospel author, the Apostle John, the two disciples address Jesus as "Rabbi," a Hebrew word that literally means "My great one." However, John was not writing to a Jewish audience, but rather to a Greek audience, so John inserts the Greek word *Didaskalos,* which means "Teacher." In both the Hebrew and Greek, what was implied by the way they responded to Jesus was that they did not only want to speak with Him on the open road, in passing, as a happenstance meeting that would result in the exchange of only a few words.

Rather, they wanted to stay with Jesus, and talk out their problems of life, and open their hearts to their troubles. What they really wanted was to be with Jesus, and the only way they could foreseeably be with Him was to know where He was staying. For our purposes, this means that the man or woman who would be a disciple of Jesus can never be satisfied with a passing word. In other words, in the deep recesses of our heart, we want to meet Jesus, not as an acquaintance in passing, but as a friend within His own house. What a different concept this is than what we are so accustomed to. Rather than inviting Jesus into my life—and my home—which is akin to declaring that He must enter my life according to my specifications, my needs, and my conditions—rather, I humbly step into His house. I leave my life behind to take up my new life in Christ.

Jesus's answer was, "Come and see!" The Jewish Rabbis had a way of using that phrase in their teaching. They would say, "Do you want to know the answer to this question? Do you want to know the solution to this problem? Come and see, and we will think about it together. Come and see, and we will do life together, and I will be with you every step of the way." When Jesus said, "Come and see!" he was inviting them, not only to come and talk, but to come and experience the life that only He could provide.

CONCLUDING THOUGHTS

IN CONCLUDING THIS LESSON (and this book), let's focus on one final and often overlooked detail of the story. Did you notice the stringent conditions under which the disciples were invited to follow Jesus? Did you happen to see the long list of things they needed to do? All the religious steps they had to take? Of course not—there weren't any! This is what I refer to as the "Supremacy of God's Grace." In other words, God's grace is everywhere you look. It is the key to unlocking the message of the Gospel.

The gift of God's grace is freely given, through faith in Jesus Christ. The Apostle Paul said it best: "It is by grace that we have been saved, through faith. And this faith is not of yourselves, it is a gift from God. It is not by works, so that no one can boast" (Ephesians 2:8–9—my translation).

And to this I believe that we can all lift our voices and proclaim:

YES and AMEN

WORKS CITED

WORKS CITED

Barclay, William. *The Acts of the Apostles Daily Study Bible*. Louisville, KY: Westminster John Knox Press, 2017.

Boyd, Gregory and Eddy Paul. *Across the Spectrum*. Grand Rapids, MI: Baker Publishing, 2009.

Chan, Francis. The Forgotten God – *Reversing Our Tragic Neglect of the Holy Spirit*. Colorado Springs, CO: David C. Cook. 2009.

Dana, H. E. *A Manual Grammar of the Greek New Testament*. New York, NY: Macmillan Publishers, 1957.

Erickson, Millard. *Christian Theology*. Grand Rapids, MI: Baker Academic, 2013.

Packer, J. I. *Knowing God*. London: Hodder & Stoughton, 1984.

Sala, Harold. *Getting Acquainted with the Holy Spirit*. Mandaluyong City, Manila. OMF Literature, INC., 2017.

Storms, Sam. *Practicing the Power*. Grand Rapids, MI: Zondervan, 2017.

Stott, John. *Baptism and Fullness*. Downers Grove, IL: InterVarsity Press, 1964.

Tennent, Timothy. *Theology in the Context of World Christianity*. Grand Rapids, MI: Zondervan, 2007.

Turner, M., in Desmond, T. Alexander. The New Dictionary of Biblical Theology – Holy Spirit. Downers Grove, IL. InterVarsity Press, 2000.

Warfield, B. B., in *Counterfeit Miracles*, as identified in Christian Theology.

Ziegler, Mollie. "Faith Unbounded" in *Christianity Today*, September 9, 2010.

ALSO FROM BESTSELLING AUTHOR GREG AMUNDSON

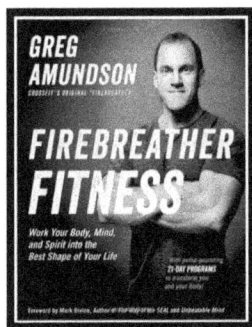

Greg Amundson's effective guides to functional fitness, nutrition, goal-setting, pain tolerance, honing purpose and focus, and exerting control over your mental state are designed to help meet any challenge. Packed with practical advice, vetted training methods, and Amundson's guided workout programs, *Firebreather Fitness* is a must-have resource for athletes, coaches, law enforcement and military professionals, and anyone interested in pursuing the high-performance life. Includes a foreword from *New York Times* bestselling author Mark Divine.

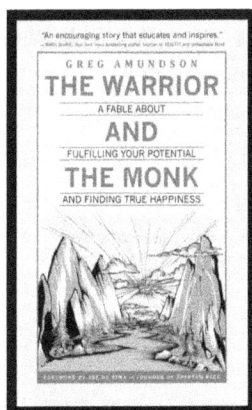

The *Warrior and The Monk* tells the extraordinary story of a young warrior who seeks the counsel of a wise monk on the universal quest to find true happiness. This is Greg Amundson's #1 Amazon multi-category bestselling book.

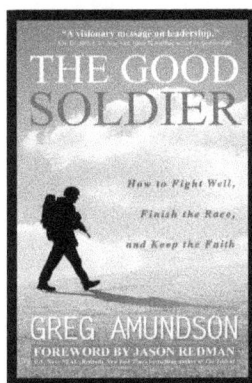

From #1 bestselling author Greg Amundson comes the nations first biblical theology on leadership through the perspective of the warrior archetype. Greg's book *The Good Soldier* opens the Bible in a fresh and relevant new way, and provides actionable steps that you can take to fight well, finish the race, and keep the faith. This is the leadership book that is redefining what it means to be a leader and a modern day warrior.

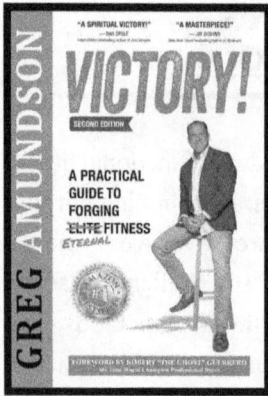

Greg Amundson's book *VICTORY* offers people of all faiths powerful strategies and practical guidelines for bringing health, happiness, fitness, and purpose into their lives and the lives of others. Renowned for his ability to merge fitness and faith, Greg offers a proven methodology for establishing life-affirming beliefs, understanding Divine wisdom, tapping into the power of prayer, integrating physical fitness with spiritual practice, and optimizing the power of mental and physical nutrition.

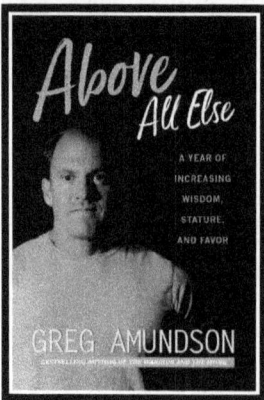

In a unique and groundbreaking new voice, Greg Amundson merges biblical truth with modern day lessons on leadership, positive psychology, and the warrior spirit. Each day of the year, you will be scripturally guided through the key principles and teachings from the Bible, resulting in a more intimate relationship with God and greater understanding of His Word. Greg's message will help you internalize disciplined practices and ways of thinking that are central to developing your full potential, and achieving your greatest dreams and goals. Greg's integration of the Mind, Body, and Spirit offers a unique perspective to keep you thriving in all aspects of your life.

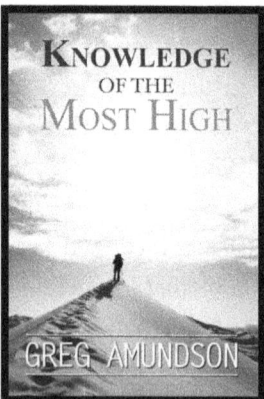

Following a three year masters degree program at Western Seminary, Greg Amundson provides the reader with an exposition of systematic theology and increased knowledge of God.

ABOUT THE AUTHOR

An alumnus of the University of California at Santa Cruz (BA Legal Theory) and Western Seminary (MA Ministry and Leadership), Greg Amundson has spent nearly twenty years in warrior professions to include assignments as a Special Weapons and Tactics Team Operator (SWAT) and Sniper in Santa Cruz County, a Captain in the United States Army, a Special Agent with the Drug Enforcement Administration (DEA) on the Southwest Border and an Agent on the highly effective Border Enforcement Security Taskforce (BEST) Team.

In addition to his extensive government work, Greg is recognized as a thought leader in the field of integrated wellness practices, and is a prolific author and speaker whose message has positively influenced the lives of thousands of spiritual seekers. A former owner of the nation's first CrossFit gym, Greg has traveled around the world teaching functional fitness and self-mastery principles for over nineteen years.

Greg is a Krav Maga Black Belt and honor graduate of the Los Angeles Police Department Handgun Instructor School (HITS). Greg currently serves as a Reserve Peace Officer and Law Enforcement Chaplain in Santa Cruz. Greg is a four-time #1 Amazon bestselling author, and the founder of Eagle Rise Publishing, a Christian focused publishing platform that has produced numerous bestselling books. Connect with Greg at www.GregoryAmundson.com.

KEYNOTES AND SEMINARS

Greg Amundson is one of North America's most electric, encouraging, and motivating professional speakers. Greg has logged more than 10,000 hours of dynamic public speaking on topics including leadership, intrinsic motivation, holistic wellness practices, functional fitness, warrior spirit, and God's Love. Greg speaks around the Country to Law Enforcement Departments on integrating disciplined warrior practices to foster increased Officer Safety while simultaneously generating stronger community relationships. A plank owner of the highly regarded Eagle Rise Speakers Bureau, Greg is renowned for his ability to transcend boundaries and speak to the heart of Spirituality. His use of captivating storytelling results in a profound and transformational learning experience.

To book Greg Amundson at your next conference or in-house event please visit www.GregoryAmundson.com.

EAGLE RISE PUBLISHING

EAGLE RISE PUBLISHING

Eagle Rise Publishing is a Christian book publisher dedicated to advancing the Kingdom of God by empowering authors to share their unique voice with the world. We offer full service "pen to publish" opportunities for aspiring authors, in addition to mentorship, powerful networking and relationship building, interior and cover design, manuscript editing and book polishing. We have published over seven #1 bestselling books, and your book can be next!

Visit www.EagleRisePublishing.com to learn more and get involved.

PODCAST

The Greg Amundson Show on iTunes is a weekly Podcast where Greg will educate and inspire you to live with passion, purpose, and a greater understanding of God's Word. Greg's use of storytelling to illuminate life changing principles and concepts is world renowned, and will become a cherished addition to spiritual seekers from all faith backgrounds.

BECOME A PATRON

If you have been blessed by the work of Greg Amundson and Eagle Rise Publishing, then there are several ways you can join our team of generous benefactors and supporters. One of the best ways to help is to post a review of this book on Amazon and share it with a friend. Reviews on Amazon and endorsements of the book on your social media platforms help new readers to find the book. You can also become a financial benefactor of Eagle Rise Publishing and help support the next generation of authors as they share their voice with the world.

Visit www.Patreon.com/GregAmundson to learn more and get involved.

www.ingramcontent.com/pod-product-compliance
Lightning Source LLC
Chambersburg PA
CBHW021152020426
42331CB00003B/21